CW01594281

My Recipe Keeper

My Recipe Keeper

Keep and record your favourite recipes

Parragon

Bath • New York • Singapore • Hong Kong • Cologne • Delhi
Melbourne • Amsterdam • Johannesburg • Auckland • Shenzhen

This edition published by Parragon in 2011

Parragon
Queen Street House
4 Queen Street
Bath BA1 1HE, UK

www.parragon.com

ISBN 978-1-4454-4364-5

Printed in China

Cover design by Talking Design
Internal design Tom Cole
Edited by Fiona Biggs

Notes for the Reader
This book uses both metric and imperial measurements. Follow the same units of measurement throughout; do not mix metric and imperial. All spoon measurements are level: teaspoons are assumed to be 5 ml, and tablespoons are assumed to be 15 ml. Unless otherwise stated, milk is assumed to be full fat, eggs and individual vegetables are medium, and pepper is freshly ground black pepper.

The times given are an approximate guide only. Preparation times differ according to the techniques used by different people and the cooking times may also vary from those given. Optional ingredients, variations or serving suggestions have not been included in the calculations.

Recipes using raw or very lightly cooked eggs should be avoided by infants, the elderly, pregnant women, convalescents and anyone suffering from an illness. Pregnant and breastfeeding women are advised to avoid eating peanuts and peanut products. Sufferers from nut allergies should be aware that some of the ready-made ingredients used in the recipes in this book may contain nuts. Always check the packaging before use.

Picture Acknowledgements
The publisher would like to thank the following for permission to reproduce copyright material on the front cover: Tulips from the Garden @ Helena Schaeder Söderberg/Getty Images
Images on pages 2 and 6 supplied courtesy of Getty Images.

Contents

72
SUCRE
SUGAR
FLOUR

Hints, tips & basic recipes

Essential kitchen equipment

Pastry boards

These are not always necessary if you have good work surfaces. However, traditionally a large board made from wood was used to knead dough. It was also traditional to have a piece of marble on which to roll out pastry because of its cool qualities and its smooth surface, which allows the pastry to be moved around easily.
If you are going to make pastry on a regular basis, it would be a sound investment to buy a specific board.

Rolling pins

In order to roll pastry well you need a heavy, smooth rolling pin.
In emergencies a milk bottle can be used, but it does not give an even rolling. Make sure the pin is of adequate length and has a smooth finish. Pins can be bought in a variety of materials: wood is traditional but you can also buy metal and glass, which are cooler. Ceramic rolling pins used to be popular but seem to have gone out of fashion now. Rolling pins with handles have also become unpopular because they reduce the surface available for rolling.

Pastry brushes

These brushes are useful for all sorts of jobs in the kitchen, such as brushing excess flour from pastry and for glazing with egg or milk. They are also used for greasing tins and brushing oil on meat and poultry before and during cooking. They are available in all shapes and sizes and in various materials. Wood is traditional but plastic brushes are now available – make sure you wash and dry them well or the bristles will start to fall out. Paint brushes are often used these days because they have a broad, flat brush, which covers the surface well. It is a good idea to have a very small one and a larger one for different tasks.

Baking beans

For years dried beans or rice have been used to weigh down greaseproof paper or baking foil. This technique is known as 'baking blind', and enables you to cook pastry without a filling until it is crisp; the filling is added later. Today you can buy ceramic and aluminium 'beans', which have a good weight and will last forever, unlike rice and beans.

Baking trays and sheets

A good, heavyweight baking tray or sheet is a must. It is not worth buying a cheap sheet because it will buckle in the oven and possibly spill the contents. Large baking sheets should have only one upturned edge so that you can slip a large or delicate item on and off easily. Trays with an edge all round are especially useful when making things like sausage rolls because they prevent the fat spilling into the oven. Make sure the trays are not too big for the oven – leave a gap all round in order for the air to circulate properly.

Cake tins

You need to decide what types of cake you are interested in making because there are so many shapes and sizes of tin available. Perhaps the best starting point is two 20-cm/8-inch sandwich tins, which are at least 2.5 cm/1 inch deep. They can be used for baking sponge cakes and Victoria sandwiches.
Loaf tins also come in many different sizes. Use one 900-g/2-lb tin and two 450-g/1-lb tins at the same time when making bread (it does not seem worth making a smaller amount of dough or having the oven on for less). They can also be used individually for tea breads and fruit terrines. Always buy the best quality you can afford: non-stick can be helpful but they still require a light coating of oil. Make sure you wash and dry them well before storing.

Bun tins

A set of 12 patty pans or a bun tray is useful for making small cakes, tarts and muffins and also for individual Yorkshire puddings. If you are going to bake quite frequently, or if you might make mince pies for Christmas, a second tray is helpful so that you can assemble one batch while one tray is in the oven.

Flan dishes

Tart tins, quiche tins, call them what you will, these items are very useful for sweet and savoury dishes. Always use steel tins, because those made from porcelain or glass do not allow the food to cook properly. Loose-based tins are the best because they allow you to remove the tin easily before serving; this is done by placing the flan on an upturned basin and allowing the ring to fall down. You can then transfer the flan on the base to a serving plate. A 20-cm/8-inch flan tin is the most useful size but if you have a large family or frequently cook for six or more people, a 30-cm/12-inch tin would be helpful. Small, individual tins are also available and these can be used for packed lunches or picnics.

Pie dishes

Pie dishes need to be quite deep with a good rim so that the pastry will be supported. They come in a number of sizes, usually oval or round, and can be glazed ceramic or glass. Some are made from enamel and tend to be oblong in shape. Larger ones need to be used with a pie funnel to support the pastry in the centre.

Wire rack

A wire rack is particularly useful if you intend to bake bread and cakes. A rack allows the steam to escape from the baked items and prevents them becoming too soggy. As soon as a cake is baked, turn it out of the tin onto an oven-gloved hand and then place it, base down, on the wire rack. This way the attractive crust on the top is maintained. Wire racks can usually be bought in rectangular or circular shapes.

Flour sieve

Sifting flour is important, not only to ensure there are no lumps but also to introduce air. A stainless steel sieve is best, of a medium size. The sieve can also be used to strain vegetables but make sure it is always cleaned and well dried after use. Plastic versions are also available. If straining acidic ingredients, such as stewed fruit, always use a non-metallic sieve to avoid a reaction between fruit juice and metal. A very small sieve is useful for sprinkling icing sugar over cakes and desserts – you could use a tea-strainer instead.

Flour dredger

A flour dredger makes it easier to sift flour onto pastry boards, pastry and rolling pins because it controls the amount of flour you use. It is also useful for sprinkling flour into casseroles to prevent lumps forming.

Mixing bowls

These bowls are available in stainless steel, copper, glass, plastic and glazed ceramic. A large plastic bowl with a rubber base is particularly good because the rubber base keeps the bowl steady when mixing. A metal bowl is good for whisking egg whites because it remains cool and the interior of the bowl can be kept absolutely smooth and clean.

Basins

You will need a variety of sizes for different tasks, such as beating eggs and whipping cream. A selection of small basins is ideal for assembling your prepared ingredients before starting to cook. Some come with lids, which is an added advantage.

Substitute ingredients

If you have decided to cook a recipe and discover that you don't have a particular ingredient, all is not lost. Use this list to discover if there is a way to substitute the item with a storecupboard standby.

If you need:	Quantity	Substitute:
Anchovies	1 fillet	1/2 tsp anchovy paste
Baking powder	1 tsp	1/4 tsp bicarbonate of soda plus 1 tsp cream of tartar
Breadcrumbs, dried	40 g/1/2 oz	35 g/1 1/4 oz cracker crumbs
Broth, chicken or beef	225 ml/8 fl oz	1 stock cube/1 tsp stock granules, dissolved in 225 m/8 fl oz boiling water
Butter	225 g/8 oz	225 g/8 oz margarine, lard or vegetable shortening/200 ml/7 fl oz vegetable oil/150 ml/5 fl oz strained bacon fat
Cornflour	1 tbsp	2 1/2 tsp arrowroot or potato starch/5 tsp rice starch
Cream, single	225 ml/8 fl oz	3 tbsp melted butter, made up to 225 ml/8 fl oz with full-fat milk (for cooking and baking only)
Eggs	1 large	2 egg yolks plus 1 tbsp cold water
Flour, self-raising	150 g/5 1/2 oz	150 g/5½ oz plain flour plus 1 tsp baking powder, 1/2 tsp salt, and 1/4 tsp bicarbonate of soda
Garlic	1 small clove	1/8 tsp garlic powder/1/2 tsp bottled garlic
Ginger, fresh	1 tbsp chopped	1/8 tsp ground ginger
Herbs, fresh	1 tsp snipped	1 tsp dried/3/4 tsp ground
Honey	225 ml/8 fl oz	280 g/10 oz granulated sugar plus 6 tbsp of the liquid called for in the recipe
Lemon juice	1 tsp	1/2 tsp vinegar
Milk		
full-fat	225 ml/8 fl oz	225 ml/8 fl oz skimmed milk, plus 2 tbsp melted butter or margarine
buttermilk	225 ml/8 fl oz	225 ml/8 fl oz natural yogurt
Mustard, prepared	1 tbsp	1 tsp mustard powder
Onion	1 small, chopped	1 tbsp instant crushed
Soured cream	225 ml/8 fl oz	225 ml/8 fl oz natural yogurt
Tomato juice	225 ml/8 fl oz	125 ml/4 fl oz tomato sauce plus 125 ml/4 fl oz water
Tomato ketchup	125 ml/4 fl oz	125 ml/4 fl oz tomato sauce plus 2 tbsp sugar and 1 tbsp vinegar
Tomato sauce	125 ml/4 fl oz	125 g/4 1/2 oz tomato purée and 125 ml/4 fl oz water
Vanilla extract	1 tsp	2.5-cm/1-inch piece of vanilla pod
Vinegar		
balsamic	1 tbsp	1 tbsp red wine vinegar plus 1/2 tsp light brown sugar
wine	1 tsp	2 tsp lemon juice
Yogurt	225 ml/8 fl oz	225 ml/8 fl oz buttermilk or 225 ml/8 fl oz full-fat milk plus 1 tbsp lemon juice

Equivalents

Sometimes it's difficult to know what the quantity specified in a recipe means in real terms; for example 1 medium lemon will provide 3 tablespoons of lemon juice. Use this ready reckoner to establish how much of any ingredient you will need.

Food	Size or quantity	Equivalent
Apples	450 g/1lb fresh	3 medium
Asparagus	450 g/1 lb fresh	12–20 spears
Breadcrumbs	25 g/1 oz fresh	1 slice bread
	25 g/1 oz dried	1 slice toast
Ginger, fresh	5-cm/2-inch piece	2 tsp crushed
Lemons	1 medium	3 tbsp juice/2–3 tsp zest
Limes	1 medium	1–2 tbsp juice/1 tsp zest
Mushrooms	85 g/3 oz dried	450 g/1 lb reconstituted
Mussels	450 g/1 lb	20 medium
Onions	450 g/1 lb	4 medium
Oranges	1 medium	6 tbsp/125 ml/4 fl oz juice/1½ tbsp zest
Peppers	450 g/1 lb	2 large
Prawns	450 g/1 lb peeled	225 g/8 oz meat
Tomatoes	450 g/1 lb fresh	3 medium
Tomato purée	125 g/4½ oz	5 tbsp
Wonton wrappers	225 g/8 oz	30 wrappers

Oven temperatures

Celsius	Fahrenheit	Gas Mark	Oven Heat
110°	225°	1/4	very cool
120°	250°	1/2	very cool
140°	275°	1	cool
150°	300°	2	cool
160°	325°	3	moderate
180°	350°	4	moderate
190°	375°	5	moderately hot
200°	400°	6	moderately hot
220°	425°	7	hot
230°	450°	8	very hot

Spoon measurements

1 teaspoon of liquid = 5 ml

1 tablespoon of liquid = 15 ml

Other measurements

Volume	
Metric	Imperial
50 ml	2 fl oz
100 ml	3 1/2 fl oz
150 ml	5 fl oz
200 ml	7 fl oz
300 ml	10 fl oz
450 ml	16 fl oz
500 ml	18 fl oz
600 ml	1 pint
700 ml	1 1/4 pints
850 ml	1 1/2 pints
1 litre	1 3/4 pints
1.5 litres	2 3/4 pints
2.8 litres	5 pints
3 litres	5 1/4 pints

Weight	
Metric	Imperial
5 g	1/8 oz
10 g	1/4 oz
25 g	1 oz
55 g	2 oz
75 g	2 3/4 oz
85 g	3 oz
100 g	3 1/2 oz
150 g	5 1/2 oz
225 g	8 oz
300 g	10 1/2 oz
450 g	1 lb
500 g	1lb 2 oz
1 kg	2 lb 4 oz
1.5 kg	3 lb 5 oz

Linear	
Metric	Imperial
2 mm	1/16 inch
3 mm	1/8 inch
5 mm	1/4 inch
8 mm	3/8 inch
1 cm	1/2 inch
2 cm	3/4 inch
2.5 cm	1 inch
5 cm	2 inches
7.5 cm	3 inches
10 cm	4 inches
20 cm	8 inches
30 cm	12 inches
46 cm	18 inches
50 cm	20 inches

Cooking methods

Try not to be daunted by the variety of cooking techniques. Enjoy experimenting, particularly with some of the increasingly popular and healthier techniques like stir-frying and griddling.

Baking

This is the term used for cooking food in the oven by dry heat, for example a baked potato or a custard. It is also the process for preparing baked goods such as cakes, biscuits and bread.

Basting

The process of moistening meat, fish or poultry while roasting in the oven. The cooking juices and fat are spooned over the food to keep it moist, to add flavour and to improve the appearance of the finished dish. If the tin becomes too dry then a little liquid, either stock or wine, can be added to the juices. Roasting vegetables are basted with oil so that they are well coated and will crisp evenly, and fried eggs are basted with hot oil to ensure the tops of the eggs are set.

Blanching

Blanching used to mean 'to whiten' and was used to whiten veal and offal. Today, however, there are two more usual meanings. Foods such as tomatoes, nuts and peaches are immersed in boiling water for a few seconds and then transferred to cold water in order to remove their skins. When preparing vegetables for freezing, the vegetables are immersed in boiling water for a short period to destroy enzymes that will spoil the flavour and texture, and then in cold water to stop the cooking process. Blanching also helps to preserve the colour of the vegetables.

Boiling

This is cooking food in a liquid at 100°C/212°F (known as boiling point). Foods cooked in this way include eggs, vegetables, rice and pasta. Although fish and meat are sometimes placed in boiling liquids, the heat is then reduced and the food is simmered to avoid loss of size, flavour and texture.

Braising

A long, slow, moist method of cooking used for cuts of meat, poultry and game that are too tough to roast. Braised food is usually cooked in one piece and the amount of liquid used is quite small. The food is browned in oil and then cooked with a quantity of vegetables in a casserole with a close-fitting lid. The dish can then be cooked on the top of the stove or in a low oven.

Casseroling

Another, more modern name for braising, taken from the name of the cooking vessel – an ovenproof casserole dish with a tight-fitting lid (this is often flameproof and can be used for the initial browning process, which cuts down on the washing up). The food is often served from the dish at the table. Casseroling also includes stews, in which the pieces of food are often cut into small pieces and more liquid is used.

Frying

The process of cooking food in hot fat. There are three main ways to fry food: pan-frying or sautéing, shallow-fat frying and deep-fat frying. Frying gives the food a delicious golden-brown colour and a wonderful flavour.

Pan-frying: A method of cooking that cooks food quickly and easily in a healthier way. Some fatty foods such as bacon and sausages can be dry-fried because they contain enough of their own fat. Small cuts of meat, poultry and fish are cooked at a high temperature in a very little fat (half oil and half butter are ideal for this – the oil allows the fat to be hot without burning and the butter adds flavour). The food is added to the hot pan, either with or without a little hot fat, and cooked on one side; the heat quickly seals the food and keeps it moist and tender. It is then turned over and cooked on the other side until cooked through. The food is then removed from the pan to a warm plate and a sauce can be made with the pan juices and a dash of wine or stock.

Shallow-fat frying: This method is used for coated foods, for example fishcakes and crumbed fish, or escalopes of meat and chicken, which are coated with flour or breadcrumbs. Use a vegetable oil such as corn oil in a shallow pan and allow enough oil to prevent the food sticking. The thicker the food, the more oil you will need. Heat the pan and the oil to a high temperature and add the food: the oil will seal the food and hence will not allow it to absorb too much fat. Once cooked on one side, turn the food over and cook on the other side. Remove it from the pan with a fish slice or a slotted spoon, shake it gently to remove excess oil and drain on kitchen paper, which will absorb any remaining fat. Serve at once while still hot.

Deep-fat frying: With this method, food is cooked while completely immersed in hot fat. The choice of fat is important because you need an oil that can be heated to a high temperature without smoking. Corn oil and soya bean oil both have high smoke points – in other words, they smoke at a higher temperature – and are good for deep frying. However, groundnut oil is the best: it has one of the highest smoke points. Foods need a protective coating when they are deep-fried – popular coverings are breadcrumbs or batter. The most usual foods to deep-fry are potato chips, seafood, fish and chicken. You will need a deep, heavy saucepan and a wire basket to lift the food out. It is quite a dangerous method of cooking because of the high temperatures. A better method is to use a thermostatically controlled electric deep-fryer.

Grilling

A very quick and easy method of cooking, which is also very healthy. The food is cooked by radiant heat, which ensures that the outside of the food is well cooked and browned while the inside remains moist. The food must be tender and of good quality. It is a good method for cooking steak, chops, chicken, burgers, sausages, whole fish, fish cutlets and fish fillets. Vegetables such as mushrooms, peppers, tomatoes and onions are also suitable. The grill must be preheated and the food brushed with oil to give protection from the fierce heat. Barbecuing is the outdoor equivalent of grilling.

Griddling

A griddle was a flat metal plate, which was used on top of the stove to cook cakes and drop scones. Nowadays the expression 'to griddle' refers to a ridged griddle pan rather like a frying pan – it has a ridged surface, which gives the food attractive brown stripes. It produces very appetizing food and is a healthy way of cooking because the food needs only a light brushing of oil. Griddling is suitable for thin steaks, chicken, salmon fillets, squid and shellfish, and for vegetables such as aubergines, courgettes, peppers, fennel and onions.

Poaching

A gentle method of cooking food in a liquid at simmering point (see Simmering, below). Poaching is suitable for small pieces of fish, particularly smoked fish such as haddock and cod, because the liquid absorbs some of the flavour and can then be used to make a sauce. Whole chickens can be poached so that the meat is succulent and tender and the well-flavoured stock can be used for soups. Whole fish such as salmon can be poached to serve whole. Poached eggs are also simple to cook. Fruit lends itself to poaching because the cooking tenderizes the fruit without causing it to lose its shape and produces a well-flavoured juice to serve with it.

Simmering

A method of cooking in liquid that is similar to boiling, but done at a lower temperature, just below boiling point. It is easy to control because you can judge it by eye. Boiling liquid has large bubbles and the surface is very agitated, but liquid at simmering point just has a gentle stream of small bubbles hardly breaking the surface. The simmering method is suitable for vegetables, chicken, fish and fruit.

Steaming

This technique involves cooking food in the steam of boiling water. Steaming is an economical method of cooking because more than one item can be cooked at a time. It is also a healthy method of cooking because there is no immersion in water and therefore very little loss of nutrients.

The most usual foods to be cooked by steaming are vegetables; often potatoes are boiled in a saucepan, a steamer is fixed over the top and other vegetables are cooked in the steam. You can buy 1–2-tiered steamers, which will fit over your saucepan and enable you to cook more than one vegetable at a time. The firmer vegetable should be at the bottom of the steamer and the more tender one at the top (where it is slightly cooler). The whole steamer is covered with a lid until the vegetables are tender.

Bamboo steamers can be used for fish, poultry and vegetables. Just bring a small amount of water to the boil in a saucepan or a wok and stack up the steamers containing the food.

Small, folding metal steamers will fit inside any saucepan. Bring 2.5 cm/1 inch of water to the boil in a saucepan, place the steamer and the vegetables in the pan, cover with the pan lid and steam until tender.

Steaming is also used for puddings. The pudding basin, well covered, is placed in a saucepan, on a trivet if you have one. The saucepan is filled halfway up with boiling water and the pudding is steamed for the correct time; the water level should be checked from time to time. Steaming gives a softer pudding than one that is baked.

Roasting

This is a method of cooking food in the oven, usually used for meat, poultry, fish and vegetables. Roasting often requires added fat to protect the food and moisten it while it is cooked at a relatively high temperature. Roasted meats are cooked in a fairly shallow roasting tin to allow the air to circulate and the surface of the meat to brown. Large, tender cuts of meat and tender poultry and game are suitable for roasting. The cooking juices can be used to make a gravy. Roasting root and Mediterranean vegetables gives them a delicious flavour.

Sautéing

The most common use of this method is preparing onions for stews or casseroles. The onions are fried in a little oil in a frying pan or a sauté pan. Because they are finely chopped they need to be kept moving to prevent them burning in the hot pan. This technique has evolved as stir-frying (see below).

Stewing

This long, slow method of cooking is used for tougher cuts of meat, older chickens and game. The meat is cut into small pieces and cooked in a large quantity of liquid. The liquid usually needs to be thickened or reduced before serving with the meat.

Stir-frying

This is a very quick way of cooking small pieces of food in a healthy and appetizing way. Stir-frying means sautéing a variety of foods together. In order to achieve this you need to prepare the meat or fish and the vegetables in advance. Although the preparation can be time-consuming, the cooking time is very short. Make sure all the pieces are the same size so that they will cook evenly. If you do not have a wok, you can use a large frying pan. Make sure everything is prepared before you start to cook because it takes very little time once started. Heat a little oil in the wok and make sure it is really hot before cooking. Only cook small quantities at a time – you need the food to fry, not steam. The most successful foods cooked in this way are thin strips of beef or pork, strips of chicken breast, prawns, scallops, slices of salmon, plaice or monkfish, and vegetables that are popular in Chinese cooking, such as pak choi, Chinese leaves, mushrooms, peppers and spring onions. Noodles are often added towards the end of the cooking time. Since this method of cooking mainly comes from the Far East, suitable flavours are added, for example ginger, soy sauce and sesame oil.

Basic nutrition

Sensible, healthy eating requires a good balance of food. A diet that contains carbohydrates, fats, protein, vitamins and minerals, plus plenty of fibre and water, will ensure that the body continues to function correctly.

Carbohydrates

This group includes all sugars, starches and fibre. Sugars are known as simple carbohydrates. They have a simple structure and can be broken down by the body easily to give a rush of instant energy. Too much sugar, however, can increase the risk of diabetes, heart disease, obesity and tooth decay.

Complex carbohydrates are present in whole grains such as corn, oats and barley and in fresh fruit and vegetables. Their complex structure takes longer to break down and provides a longer, steadier flow of energy.

Fibre

Fibre cannot be digested, but it is still very important in the diet because it provides bulk to assist the passage of the food through the intestines. A good intake of fibre thus helps prevent constipation.

Protein

Protein is essential for growth and repair of the body, and any excess can be used to provide energy. Proteins have a complex structure and are composed of amino acids. The ones that are necessary for the human body are known as essential amino acids. These are present in the correct ratio in animal proteins and have a high biological value. Vegetable proteins, known as incomplete proteins, provide only some of the essential amino acids and therefore need to be eaten in combinations that complement each other in order to provide the correct balance of amnio acids.

Fats

Oils and fats are present in the diet as the most concentrated form of energy. Not all fats are bad. Bad fats are the saturated fatty acids found in animal fats such as butter and cheese, and in animal products such as sausages, bacon, pork, lamb, beefburgers, eggs and full-fat milk. Saturated fats are thought to increase blood cholesterol levels and therefore to be responsible for heart disease. Polyunsaturated and monounsaturated fatty acids are believed to reduce cholesterol levels; these are available in corn oil, olive oil, soya and sunflower oils, and nut oils (not coconut).

Vitamins

Vitamins help to regulate important body processes. Apart from vitamin D, all the vitamins must be supplied in the diet because the body is unable to manufacture them.

Vitamins are either water-soluble or fat-soluble. Water-soluble vitamins include vitamins B_1, B_2, B_6 and B_{12} and vitamin C; the fat-soluble vitamins include vitamins A, D, E and K. Vitamins may be taken as supplements but they are expensive, and if you have a well-balanced diet they should be unnecessary.

Minerals

Minerals are inorganic elements needed by the body in very small amounts. Calcium, phosphorus and magnesium are important constituents of bones and teeth; sodium, chloride, magnesium, potassium and phosphorus are present as soluble salts in body fluids; iron, phosphorus and zinc aid the process of releasing energy. Trace elements, such as copper, fluoride, selenium, iodine, manganese, chromium and cobalt, are also needed, but in smaller amounts. A well-balanced diet should provide all of these elements. Supplements are widely available but should be used with discretion.

Water

Water is needed for transporting nutrients, for digestion, for circulation, for body heat regulation and for excretion. You need to drink at least eight 225 ml/8 fl oz glasses of water each day for proper body function and to avoid feelings of lethargy.

Preparation techniques

Baking blind
Pastry cases can be baked without a filling so that the pastry is well cooked. The tin or dish is lined with pastry and then with baking paper or foil, which is weighed down with baking beans (actual dried beans or ceramic or metal ones) to prevent the pastry bubbling up while cooking. The beans and foil are then removed and the pastry case cooked for a while longer to dry it out.

Beating
This makes food lighter by incorporating air, using a fork, a wooden spoon or an electric mixer. It is most often used for eggs, for omelettes and for cakes, beating together the butter and sugar (also known as creaming). It is also used to mix sauces or custards, to make the consistency smooth and remove lumps.

Blending
Blending means combining ingredients together, usually with a spoon. You can blend cornflour and water to a smooth paste, for example before using to thicken soups and stews. Blending also refers to mixing soups and purées in a blender to reduce them to a smooth liquid and remove any lumps.

Crimping
This means to decorate the edges of a pie in order to ensure the edges are well sealed. This is done by pinching the pastry with a finger and thumb of one hand and pressing with the first finger of the other hand, giving a fluted edge. Crimping is also used purely decoratively on shortbread or plate pies.

Cutting
Cutting is a basic technique used to prepare meat, fruit and vegetables. Using a knife correctly is an important step in preparing food. Food that is correctly prepared will cook more evenly and have a more attractive appearance. A good knife and a firm board are essential. Make sure the knife is sharp because blunt knives cause accidents. Use the correct knife for the task, for example a bread knife for bread and a serrated knife for tomatoes.

Chopping
This is one step on from cutting. The food is divided into small pieces by more than one cut. To chop an onion, for example, halve the onion from the top down through the stem and root, then place the flat side of one half down on the board and cut the onion from root to stem into fine slices. Turn the knife and slice through the onion the other way, ensuring that you have even, small pieces. Chopping herbs is another important skill. Hold the tip of the blade down with one hand and raise the handle of the knife up and down with your other hand as you chop into the herb, moving from left to right and back again so that you work all over the food. Chopping can be done roughly or finely: roughly means pieces of food about 1 cm/½ inch; finely means much smaller pieces. It is important to chop all the pieces to an even size. Sometimes a recipe might ask for food to be diced: dice are pieces not only of the same size but of a regular shape; for example diced cucumber should be small cubes.

Crushing
This technique is used for herbs and garlic and for making biscuit crumbs for cheesecakes or flan cases. To crush garlic, simply press down on the garlic using the flat side of a knife blade. You can also use a garlic press. To make biscuit crumbs, put the biscuits in a large plastic bag, close the end of the bag securely and then crush the biscuits with a rolling pin.

Dredging
Dredging means sprinkling pastry with flour before rolling it out. The board and the rolling pin should be lightly floured to prevent the pastry sticking to them. The term can also be used for sugar and cocoa powder, for example to dredge a cake with icing sugar.

Folding in
The term used to describe how to incorporate flour into a cake mixture. It is a gentle movement, made using a metal spoon or a plastic spatula, cutting through the mixture in a figure-of-eight movement, enabling the flour to combine without losing the air already incorporated. The

same term is used in reference to meringues and soufflés.

Glazing

A glaze is a finish that is brushed on to pastry and bread before baking. It can be prepared using milk, beaten egg, or water and sugar.

Grating

A grater is used to shred food into small particles. A box grater is useful because it has different-sized surfaces and can produce medium and fine gratings. A food processor can grate food very quickly and is useful if you have a large quantity to prepare.

Grinding

Grinding reduces foods to a powder or very small particles. Spices can be ground in a mortar with a pestle or in a coffee grinder that has been reserved for that purpose. A food processor is good for grinding nuts and chocolate.

Kneading

This is a technique used in breadmaking. The dough is kneaded to develop the gluten in the flour so that it will hold its shape when risen. The dough is pummelled on a lightly floured board until it is smooth and elastic. Kneading uses the heel of the hand to pull and stretch the dough. It can also be done in a free-standing mixer using a dough hook.

Knocking back

This describes the process whereby the air is knocked out of the bread dough after its first rising and is then gently kneaded for 1 minute before a second rising or 'proving'.

Marinating

This is soaking food in a marinade, which will tenderize it and add flavour. Marinating is used for meat, poultry and game. The meat is covered with a mixture of oil, wine or vinegar and flavourings such as garlic and herbs. The food can be marinated for a few hours or a few days. During cooking, the marinade can be used to baste the food.

Mincing

This means chopping food very finely, using a hand or electric mincer. A food processor can also be used.

Rubbing in

This is a method of making cakes, pastry and bread, where the fat is rubbed into the flour using the tips of the fingers, lifting the flour high out of the basin so that the air will be trapped in the mixture. This makes the mixture lighter.

Scoring

This involves making light cuts on the surface of food to help it cook more quickly, to reduce fat and also to make the food look more attractive.

Sieving

This is a method of rubbing cooked food through a sieve, using a wooden spoon, to form a purée. Sieving can also refer to straining vegetables after cooking to remove the cooking water.

Sifting

This is the same as sieving but refers to dry ingredients, for example sugar and flour, to remove lumps and to add air to the mixture. With these ingredients, there is no need to push them through with a wooden spoon.

Tenderizing

This is beating raw meat with a rolling pin or a meat hammer to soften the fibres and make the meat tender before frying or grilling.

Trussing

This is the technique used for poultry and game whereby the bird is pulled into shape and then held with skewers or by string to maintain its shape during cooking.

Whisking

This is another method used to incorporate air, but it is usually used for a lighter mixture, for example egg whites or cream. To make the task easier and more efficient, you really need an electric mixer for whisking. However, a wire whisk used in a large mixing bowl with lots of energy can perform the task adequately.

Kitchen hygiene

Buying food

Always buy from a reputable source where you have confidence in their food handling techniques.

Buy the freshest foods and the best quality possible.

Storage

Keep food for as short a time as possible before cooking or serving, and ensure that it is stored at a safe temperature. A refrigerator should operate at below 5°C/41°F, so keep a thermometer in the refrigerator and check it from time to time to ensure it is working satisfactorily. Adjust the thermostat when necessary.

Cover all food in the refrigerator with clingfilm so that one food does not contaminate another. Be especially aware of any meat products, which might leak blood onto other foods.

Check 'use by' dates on packs of food before cooking.

Defrost frozen food thoroughly before cooking. Defrost it overnight in the refrigerator rather than at room temperature.

Preparation

Carefully wash any foods that need cleaning and dry well with kitchen paper – this is more hygienic than using a cloth.

Wash your hands frequently with soap when preparing food. Use a separate hand towel, not a tea towel, to dry them.

Keep work surfaces clean and use different chopping boards for cooked and uncooked foods, particularly meats. Wash them well and then rinse thoroughly with diluted bleach between each use. Wash knives and other utensils in hot water and soap between each use.

Keep dish cloths clean and make sure that you change them often. Keep waste bins covered and empty them frequently, disinfecting regularly.

Cooking

Make sure food is cooked thoroughly and serve it piping hot as soon as practicable.

When cooked food needs to be kept, make sure it is cooled quickly, covered and placed in the refrigerator as soon as possible. It is when food is kept at room temperature that food-poisoning bacteria multiply, so avoid keeping foods for long periods at this temperature.

Reheat food only once; if it is not then used up, throw it away. It is safer than risking illness. However, never reheat a marinade, especially one that has been used for marinating meat.

Basic recipes

Vegetable stock

Makes about 2 litres/3½ pints

- 2 tbsp sunflower oil
- 115 g/4 oz onion, finely chopped
- 40 g/1½ oz leek, finely chopped
- 115 g/4 oz carrot, finely chopped
- 4 celery sticks, finely chopped
- 85 g/3 oz fennel, finely chopped
- 1 small tomato, finely chopped
- 2.25 litres/4 pints water
- 1 bouquet garni

Heat the oil in a large saucepan. Add the onion and leek and cook over a low heat, stirring occasionally, for 5 minutes, until soft. Add the remaining vegetables, cover and cook for 10 minutes. Add the water and bouquet garni, bring to the boil and simmer for 20 minutes.

Strain the stock into a bowl, leave to cool, cover and store in the refrigerator. Use immediately or freeze in portions for up to 3 months.

Fish stock

Makes about 1.3 litres/2¼ pints

- 650 g/1 lb 7 oz white fish heads, bones and trimmings, rinsed
- 1 onion, sliced
- 2 celery sticks, chopped
- 1 carrot, sliced
- 1 bay leaf
- 4 fresh parsley sprigs
- 4 black peppercorns
- ½ lemon, sliced
- 1.3 litres/2¼ pints water
- 125 ml/4 fl oz dry white wine

Cut out and discard the gills from any fish heads, then place the heads, bones and trimmings in a saucepan. Add all the remaining ingredients and gradually bring to the boil, skimming off the foam that rises to the surface. Partially cover and simmer for 25 minutes.

Strain the stock without pressing down on the contents of the sieve. Leave to cool, cover and store in the refrigerator. Use immediately or freeze in portions for up to 3 months.

Chicken stock

Makes about 2.5 litres/4½ pints

- 1.3 kg/3 lb chicken wings and necks
- 2 onions, cut into wedges
- 4 litres/7 pints water
- 2 carrots, coarsely chopped
- 2 celery sticks, coarsely chopped
- 10 fresh parsley sprigs
- 4 fresh thyme sprigs
- 2 bay leaves
- 10 black peppercorns

Put the chicken wings and necks and the onions in a large saucepan and cook over a low heat, stirring frequently, until lightly browned.

Add the water and stir well to scrape off any sediment from the base of the pan. Gradually bring to the boil, skimming off the foam that rises to the surface. Add all the remaining ingredients, partially cover and simmer for 3 hours.

Strain the stock into a bowl, leave to cool, cover and store in the refrigerator. When cold, remove and discard the layer of fat from the surface. Use immediately or freeze in portions for up to 6 months.

Beef stock

Makes about 1.7 litres/3 pints

- 1 kg/2 lb 4 oz beef marrow bones, sawn into 7.5-cm/3-inch pieces
- 650 g/1 lb 7 oz stewing steak in a single piece
- 2.8 litres/5 pints water
- 4 cloves
- 2 onions, halved
- 2 celery sticks, coarsely chopped
- 8 black peppercorns
- 1 bouquet garni

Place the bones in the base of a large saucepan and put the meat on top. Add the water and gradually bring to the boil, skimming off any foam that rises to the surface.

Press a clove into each onion half and add to the pan with the celery, peppercorns and bouquet garni. Partially cover and simmer for 3 hours. Remove the meat and simmer for a further hour.

Strain the stock into a bowl, cover and store in the refrigerator. When cold, remove and discard the layer of fat from the surface. Use immediately or freeze in portions for up to 6 months.

Béchamel sauce

Makes about 350 ml/12 fl oz

300 ml/10 fl oz milk

1 small onion, studded with 2–3 cloves

1 mace blade

1 fresh bay leaf

3–4 white or black peppercorns

1 small piece carrot, peeled

2 tbsp unsalted butter or margarine

35 g/1¼ oz plain flour

salt and pepper

Pour the milk into a small heavy-based saucepan with a lid. Add the onion, mace, bay leaf, peppercorns and carrot. Heat over a gentle heat and slowly bring to just boiling point. Remove from the heat, cover and set aside for at least 30 minutes. Strain and reheat until warm.

Melt the butter in a separate small saucepan and sprinkle in the flour. Cook over a gentle heat, stirring constantly with a wooden spoon, for 2 minutes. Remove from the heat and gradually stir in the warmed infused milk, adding a little at a time and stirring until the milk has been incorporated before adding more. When all the milk has been added, return to the heat and cook, stirring, until thick, smooth and glossy. Add salt and pepper to taste and serve.

Beurre blanc

Makes about 125 ml/4 fl oz

2 tbsp finely chopped shallot

2 tbsp white wine vinegar

115 g/4 oz unsalted butter

salt and pepper

Put the shallot in a small heavy-based saucepan with the vinegar and salt and pepper to taste. Bring to the boil and boil for 2–3 minutes until reduced to about 2 teaspoons. Add 2 tablespoons of the butter and beat vigorously with a wire whisk while bringing to the boil. Remove from the heat and whisk in the remaining butter, a piece at a time. When all the butter has been added, check and adjust the seasoning if necessary, and serve.

Greek garlic sauce

Makes about 225 ml/8 fl oz

115 g/4 oz whole blanched almonds
3 tbsp fresh white breadcrumbs
2 large garlic cloves, crushed
2 tsp lemon juice
150 ml/5 fl oz extra virgin olive oil
4 tbsp hot water
salt and pepper

Put the almonds in a food processor and blend until finely ground. Add the breadcrumbs, garlic, lemon juice, and salt and pepper to taste, and mix well together. With the machine running, very slowly pour in the oil to form a smooth, thick mixture. When all the oil has been added, blend in the water. Turn the mixture into a bowl and chill for at least 2 hours.

Aïoli

Makes about 300 ml/10 fl oz

1 large egg yolk
1 tbsp white wine vinegar or lemon juice
2 large garlic cloves, peeled and crushed
5 tbsp extra virgin olive oil
5 tbsp sunflower oil
salt and pepper

Put the egg yolk, vinegar, garlic, and salt and pepper to taste in a bowl and whisk until all the ingredients are well blended. Add the olive oil, then the sunflower oil, drop by drop at first, and then in a slow, steady stream until thick and smooth.

Hollandaise sauce

Makes about 225 ml/8 fl oz

2 tbsp white wine vinegar
1 tbsp water
2 egg yolks
115 g/4 oz unsalted butter, slightly softened and diced
lemon juice (optional)
salt and pepper

Pour the vinegar and water into a small heavy-based saucepan and bring to the boil. Boil for 3 minutes, or until reduced by half. Remove from the heat and leave to cool slightly.

Put the egg yolks in a heatproof bowl and beat in the cooled vinegar water. Set over a saucepan of gently simmering water, ensuring that the base of the bowl does not touch the simmering water. Cook, stirring constantly, until the mixture thickens slightly and lightly coats the back of the spoon. Keeping the water simmering, add the butter, a piece at a time, until the sauce is thick, smooth and glossy. Add a little lemon juice and salt and pepper to taste and serve warm.

Tartare sauce

Makes about 300 ml/10 fl oz

- 2 large egg yolks
- 2 tsp Dijon mustard
- 2 tbsp lemon juice or white wine vinegar
- about 300 ml/10 fl oz sunflower oil
- 10 cornichons, finely chopped
- 1 tbsp capers, finely chopped
- 1 tbsp finely chopped parsley
- salt and pepper

Whiz the egg yolks with the Dijon mustard, and salt and pepper to taste, in a food processor or blender or by hand. Add the lemon juice and whiz again. With the motor still running or still beating, add the oil, drop by drop at first. When the sauce begins to thicken, the oil can then be added in a slow, steady stream. Stir in the cornichons, capers and parsley. Taste and adjust the seasoning with extra salt and pepper and lemon juice if necessary. If the sauce seems too thick, slowly add 1 tablespoon of hot water. Use at once or store in an airtight container in the refrigerator for up to 1 week.

Mayonnaise

Makes about 300 ml/10 fl oz

- 2 egg yolks
- 150 ml/5 fl oz sunflower oil
- 150 ml/5 fl oz olive oil
- 1 tbsp white wine vinegar
- 2 tsp Dijon mustard
- salt and pepper

Beat the egg yolks with a pinch of salt. Combine the sunflower oil and the olive oil in a jug. Gradually add one quarter of the oil mixture to the beaten egg, a drop at a time, beating constantly with a whisk or electric mixer. Beat in the vinegar, then continue adding the combined oils in a steady stream, beating constantly. Stir in the mustard and season to taste with salt and pepper.

Slim-line dressing

Makes about 300 ml/10 fl oz

300 ml/10 fl oz low-fat natural yogurt

1 tsp English mustard

2–3 tbsp lemon juice

4 tsp sunflower oil

salt and pepper, to taste

Put all the ingredients into a food processor and process on medium speed until thoroughly combined.

Garlic, chilli & oregano oil

Makes about 225 ml/8 fl oz

5 garlic cloves, halved lengthways

2 tbsp deseeded and chopped red hot chilli

1 tsp dried oregano

225 ml/8 fl oz rapeseed oil

Preheat the oven to 150°C/300°F/Gas Mark 2. Combine the garlic, chilli and oregano with the oil in an ovenprooof glass measuring jug. Place on a glass pie plate in the centre of the oven and heat for 1½–2 hours. The temperature of the oil should reach 120°C/250°F.

Remove from the oven, allow to cool, then strain through muslin into a clean jar. Store, covered, in the refrigerator. You can also leave the garlic and chilli pieces in the oil and strain before using.

Tomato dressing

Serves 2–4

2 tbsp balsamic vinegar, or red or white wine vinegar

4–6 tbsp extra virgin olive oil

1 tsp Dijon mustard

pinch of caster sugar

1 tbsp torn fresh basil leaves

1 tbsp chopped sun-dried tomatoes

salt and pepper

Place all the ingredients in a screw-top jar, secure the top and shake well. Alternatively, beat all the ingredients together in a small bowl. Use as much oil as you like.

If you have just salad leaves to dress, 4 tablespoons of oil will be sufficient, but if you have heavier ingredients such as potatoes, you will need about 6 tablespoons of oil.
Use the dressing at once. If you want to store it, do not add the herbs – it will then keep for 3–4 days in the refrigerator.

Basic dough recipe

The method used is basically the same for all yeast breads, although individual steps may vary according to the recipe.

Makes 1 loaf

- 675 g/1$^1/_2$ lb strong plain bread flour
- 2 tsp salt
- 2 tsp easy-blend dried yeast
- about 450 ml/16 fl oz hand-hot water
- 2 tbsp olive oil or 25 g/1 oz butter

Sift the flour and salt into a large bowl. Stir in the yeast and make a well in the centre. Pour in the liquid and mix to a soft, sticky dough.

Turn out the dough onto a lightly floured work surface and begin kneading by folding the dough over on top of itself and pushing away with the heel of your hand – do not be afraid to be quite forceful. Keep kneading, giving the dough a quarter turn as you do so, for 10 minutes, or until the dough is very smooth and elastic and no longer sticky. Alternatively, knead the dough in an electric mixer fitted with a dough hook for 6-8 minutes.

Form the dough into a ball and put in a lightly oiled bowl. Rub a little oil over the surface of the dough to prevent it drying out and cover loosely with clingfilm or slide the bowl inside a clean plastic carrier bag. Leave to rise in a warm place for 1 hour, or until doubled in size.

When the dough has increased to double its original size, turn out onto a lightly floured work surface and knock back.

Shape the dough as required and place in a lightly greased baking tin or tray. If placing in a tin, the dough should half-fill the tin.

Cover loosely again and leave to rise (prove) for a second time until doubled in size.

Bake in a hot oven. To test if the bread is cooked, turn out of the tin and tap the base. The loaf should sound hollow. Leave to cool on a wire rack.

Pizza dough

Makes 2 x 25-cm/10-inch pizzas

- 225 g/8 oz plain flour, plus extra for dusting
- 1 tsp salt
- 6 tbsp hand-hot water
- 2 tbsp olive oil, plus extra for oiling
- 1 tsp easy-blend dried yeast

Sift the flour with the salt into a large, warmed bowl and make a well in the centre. Add the water, oil and yeast to the well. Using a wooden spoon or your hands, gradually mix, drawing the flour from the sides, to form a dough.

Turn out onto a lightly floured work surface and knead for 5 minutes, or until smooth and elastic. Form the dough into a ball, put in a clean, lightly oiled bowl and cover with oiled clingfilm. Leave in a warm place to rise for 1 hour, or until doubled in size.

Turn out the dough onto a lightly floured work surface and knock back. Knead briefly before shaping into 2 pizza bases.

Shortcrust pastry

225 g/8 oz plain flour

115 g/4 oz butter

2–3 tbsp cold water

Sift the flour into a bowl. Cut the butter into small cubes and add to the flour. Rub in using your fingertips, lifting your hands high above the bowl to incorporate more air. The mixture will resemble fine breadcrumbs when the butter has been fully rubbed in.

Stir in any additional flavourings, if using, such as ground nuts or cheese, or sugar for sweet pastry.

Add the water and use your fingers to bring the pastry together. Turn out the dough onto a lightly floured work surface and knead very lightly. Ideally, the pastry should be wrapped in foil or clingfilm and chilled in the refrigerator for 30 minutes to allow the pastry to 'relax', which helps prevent it shrinking when baked.

Roll out the dough on a lightly floured work surface. Turn the pastry as you roll.

Use as required, then allow the pastry to relax again in a cool place for 15-30 minutes before baking. This is especially important if you have not previously relaxed the pastry. Bake in a hot oven for 15–20 minutes until set. The temperature may then be reduced.

Shortcrust pastry can be made in a food processor, which helps to keep it cooler than warm hands can. Put the flour and butter in the processor and process until the mixture resembles fine breadcrumbs. The liquid can then be added to the machine, processing until the pastry comes together. Alternatively, for greater control, tip the flour and butter mixture into a bowl and add the liquid by hand.

Puff pastry

350 g/12 oz plain flour

175 g/6 oz butter

8 tbsp cold water

Sift the flour into a bowl and rub in a quarter of the butter. Add the water and use your fingers to bring the pastry together. Knead briefly to form a smooth dough. Put in a polythene bag and chill in the refrigerator for 30 minutes.

Roll out the remaining butter between 2 sheets of clingfilm to form a block about 1 cm/½ inch thick.

Roll out the dough to a square about 4 times the size of the block of butter.

Put the block of butter in the centre of the dough and fold over the corners of the dough to completely enclose the butter. Roll out the dough into a rectangle three times as long as it is wide.

Fold a third of the dough over to cover the middle third, then fold the remainder over the top.

Give the dough a half turn, roll out to form another rectangle and fold again as before. Repeat the initial rolling and folding 6 times in total, chilling the dough frequently between rolling. Leave to relax for a final 30 minutes, then use as required. Trim the folded edges of the pastry before using to assist the rising. Bake in a hot oven. The pastry should rise 6–8 times its original height.

Soups

Tomato soup

Serves 4

55 g/2 oz butter
1 small onion, finely chopped
450 g/1 lb tomatoes, coarsely chopped
1 bay leaf
3 tbsp plain flour
600 ml/1 pint milk
salt and pepper
sprigs of fresh basil, to garnish

Melt half the butter in a saucepan. Add the onion and cook over a low heat, stirring occasionally, for 5–6 minutes until soft. Add the tomatoes and bay leaf and cook, stirring occasionally, for 15 minutes, or until pulpy.

Meanwhile, melt the remaining butter in another saucepan. Add the flour and cook, stirring constantly, for 1 minute. Remove the pan from the heat and gradually stir in the milk. Return to the heat, season with salt and pepper and bring to the boil, stirring constantly. Continue to cook, stirring, until smooth and thick.

When the tomatoes are pulpy, remove the pan from the heat. Discard the bay leaf and pour the tomato mixture into a blender or food processor. Process until smooth, then push through a sieve into a clean saucepan. Bring the tomato mixture to the boil, then gradually stir it into the milk mixture. Season to taste with salt and pepper. Ladle into warmed bowls, garnish with basil sprigs and serve immediately.

Chunky vegetable soup

Serves 6

2 carrots, sliced

1 onion, diced

1 garlic clove, crushed

350 g/12 oz new potatoes, diced

2 celery sticks, sliced

115 g/4 oz closed-cup mushrooms, quartered

400 g/14 oz canned chopped tomatoes

600 ml/1 pint vegetable stock

1 bay leaf

1 tsp dried mixed herbs or 1 tbsp chopped fresh mixed herbs

85 g/3 oz sweetcorn kernels, frozen or canned, drained

55 g/2 oz green cabbage, shredded

pepper

sprigs of fresh basil, to garnish

Put the carrots, onion, garlic, potatoes, celery, mushrooms, tomatoes and stock into a large saucepan. Stir in the bay leaf and herbs. Bring to the boil, then reduce the heat, cover and simmer for 25 minutes.

Add the sweetcorn and cabbage and return to the boil. Reduce the heat, cover and simmer for 5 minutes, or until the vegetables are tender. Remove and discard the bay leaf. Season to taste with pepper.

Ladle into warmed bowls, garnish with basil and serve immediately.

Chicken noodle soup

Serves 4–6

2 skinless chicken breasts

1.2 litres/2 pints Chicken Stock (see page 21)

3 carrots, peeled and sliced into 5-mm/¼-inch slices

85 g/3 oz dried vermicelli (or other small noodles)

salt and pepper

fresh tarragon leaves, to garnish

Place the chicken breasts in a large saucepan, add the stock and bring to a simmer. Cook for 25–30 minutes. Skim any foam from the surface if necessary. Remove the chicken from the stock and keep warm.

Continue to simmer the stock, add the carrots and vermicelli and cook for 4–5 minutes.

Thinly slice or shred the chicken breasts and place in warmed serving dishes.

Season the soup to taste with salt and pepper and pour over the chicken. Serve at once, garnished with the tarragon.

Creamy mushroom soup

Serves 4–6

50 g/1¾ oz butter

1 onion, chopped

700 g/1 lb 9 oz button mushrooms, coarsely chopped

850 ml/1½ pints Vegetable Stock (see page 20)

3 tbsp chopped fresh tarragon, plus extra to garnish

150 ml/5 fl oz crème fraîche

salt and pepper

Melt half the butter in a large saucepan. Add the onion and cook gently for 10 minutes until soft. Add the remaining butter and the mushrooms and cook for 5 minutes, or until the mushrooms are browned.

Stir in the stock and tarragon, bring to the boil, then reduce the heat and leave to simmer gently for 20 minutes. Transfer to a food processor or blender and process until smooth. Return the soup to the rinsed-out pan.

Stir in the crème fraîche and add salt and pepper to taste. Reheat the soup gently until hot. Ladle into warmed serving bowls and garnish with chopped tarragon. Serve immediately.

Salads & vegetables

Salad leaves and vegetables

Take a fresh look at salads and you'll see there are a lot of exciting developments in the salad bowl. Banished forever is the image of salads as dull diet food consisting of little more than limp lettuce and soggy, flavourless tomatoes.

Today, salads are among the ultimate health foods. They can contain an exciting variety of colourful, delicious and satisfying ingredients that provide the nutrients essential for healthy living. You'll find plenty of inspiration in this chapter for a range of healthy salads for all occasions, from light lunches and family meals to stylish dinner parties.

Salads are versatile enough to cater for vegetarians and meat-eaters alike. Meat, seafood and poultry are ideal salad ingredients, along with the perhaps more commonly used lettuce and other leaves, vegetables, fruit, herbs, nuts, seeds, grains, pulses and cheese. And with so many ingredients to choose from, salads can be as simple and light or complex and filling as you like. They also have an added bonus in that they are versatile enough to fit easily into all your meal plans, from starters through to desserts.

Inside this chapter you will find a selection of classic salads, including the all-time favourite Caesar Salad. And if the idea of chicken salad no longer excites you because you have been making the same recipe for as long as you can remember, try a Waldorf Chicken Salad. You'll never think of chicken salad as boring again!

Bowls of goodness

It wasn't long ago that when 'salads' and 'health' were linked it was in the context of weight-reducing diets that were restrictive and ultimately unsatisfying. Today, however, salads are a delicious component of a healthy diet, giving you endless variety at mealtimes without long hours in the kitchen.

With fresh produce from all corners of the globe readily available in supermarkets and gourmet food shops, you can enjoy a variety of salads all year round but, remember, salads are at their most flavoursome and nutritious when made with seasonal produce in its prime.

A salad a day can go a long way to help you meet the minimum daily target of five portions of fruit and vegetables. Served alongside a filling bowl of pasta or a plate of hot or cold roast meat, salads also make great accompaniments.

So, if you regularly fall back on the old favourite of just tossing a few green leaves with a simple oil-and-vinegar dressing, it's definitely time to think again. It's very easy to mix and match ingredients and the choice has never been greater. And don't make the mistake of thinking all salad ingredients have to be raw, either. Adding small amounts of cooked meat, poultry and seafood to lettuce leaves and other vegetables will give you a satisfying and healthy meal at any time.

Cooked vegetables also make good salad ingredients. Grilled peppers, fried aubergines, blanched beans and peas are just some of the cooked vegetables that add flavour and an extra dimension.

Colourful greens

Even with so many ingredients to choose from, salad greens still provide the backbone of many popular salads. Take a look around your supermarket or greengrocer's and you'll see leaves in many colours and textures, ranging from pearly, pale white chicory to bright red and white radicchio. They also have a variety of flavours, from robust and peppery to sweet, nutty and mild.

The greater the variety of leaves you include in your salad, the more interesting it will be, and the more nutrients it will contain. When you select salad leaves, remember that the darker coloured ones, such as spinach leaves, contain more beta-carotene, which helps fight some forms of cancer and other illnesses. Leafy green vegetables are also excellent sources of fibre.

Try these new and familiar greens to add variety to your salad bowl:

- Beet greens – distinctive with their ruby-red stalks, these soft leaves are mildly flavoured.

- Cos lettuce – Caesar Salad (see page 46) simply wouldn't be Caesar Salad without these long, crisp leaves. Cos comes in a large, compact head with long, crisp leaves that have a sweet nutty flavour.

- Lamb's lettuce – also known as corn salad or mâche, these tender leaves have a mild, slightly nutty flavour.

- Mesclun or mesclum – now sold in supermarkets, this French mix of leaves can include chervil, dandelion, oakleaf lettuce and rocket. Just add dressing and toss.

- Mizuna – from the Far East, this winter green has a full peppery flavour. Its pointy green leaves add visual interest to salads, too.

- Nasturtiums – use both the colourful flowers and peppery leaves in salads.

- Radicchio – there is nothing like the bright red and white leaves of this member of the bitter chicory family to enliven autumn and early winter salads. It has a crisp texture and a nutty, peppery flavour.

- Red chard – like beet greens, these fibre-rich leaves have bright red stalks and sometimes the leaves are tinged red as well.

- Rocket – known for their pronounced peppery flavour, these dark green leaves perk up many salads. They are popular in Italian salads. Substitute watercress if you can't find rocket.

Keep it fresh

Good salads are made with good ingredients, and freshness is all-important. Because of the leaves' high water content, they are very perishable, so buy them as close as possible to serving. Let your eyes guide you – fresh leaves look fresh. They aren't tinged with brown, nor are they wilted or slimy.

When you get salad ingredients home, give them a rinse in cold water, then spin in a centrifugal salad spinner or use a tea towel to pat them dry. Never leave them to soak in a sink of cold water because all the water-soluble vitamins and minerals will escape.

Use leafy ingredients as soon as possible, although most will keep for up to four days in a sealed container in the fridge. Once you open bags of prepared leaves, however, they should be used within 24 hours. You can prepare salad greens several hours in advance and store in the fridge, but do not dress until just before serving, because the acid in most dressings causes the leaves to wilt and become unappetizing.

Vegetable roast

Roasted vegetables are the perfect accompaniment to roast or grilled meat and fish. Try Perfect Roast Potatoes (see page 50) and you'll never roast potatoes any other way. Winter vegetables, such as parsnips and carrots, taste particularly good when roasted, and it's a great way to liven up these root vegetables. which are often regarded as dull and uninspiring.

Caesar salad

Serves 4

1 large egg

2 cos lettuces or
3 Little Gem lettuces

6 tbsp olive oil

2 tbsp lemon juice

8 canned anchovy fillets, drained and roughly chopped

85 g/3 oz fresh Parmesan cheese shavings

salt and pepper

Garlic croûtons

4 tbsp olive oil

2 garlic cloves

5 slices white bread, crusts removed, cut into 1-cm/½-inch cubes

Bring a small, heavy-based saucepan of water to the boil.

Meanwhile, make the croûtons. Heat the oil in a heavy-based frying pan. Add the garlic and diced bread and cook, stirring and tossing frequently, for 4–5 minutes, or until the bread is crispy and golden all over. Remove from the frying pan with a slotted spoon and drain on kitchen paper.

While the bread is frying, add the egg to the boiling water and cook for 1 minute, then remove from the saucepan and reserve.

Arrange the lettuce leaves in a salad bowl. Mix the oil and lemon juice together, then season to taste with salt and pepper. Crack the egg into the dressing and whisk to blend. Pour the dressing over the lettuce leaves, toss well, then add the croûtons and chopped anchovies and toss the salad again. Sprinkle with the cheese shavings and serve.

Traditional Greek salad

Serves 4

200 g/7 oz Greek feta cheese

½ head Webbs lettuce or 1 lettuce such as cos or escarole, shredded or sliced

4 tomatoes, quartered

½ cucumber, sliced

12 Greek black olives, stoned

2 tbsp chopped fresh herbs such as oregano, flat-leaf parsley, mint or basil

Dressing

6 tbsp extra virgin olive oil

2 tbsp fresh lemon juice

1 garlic clove, crushed

pinch of sugar

salt and pepper, to taste

Make the dressing by whisking together all the ingredients in a small bowl. Set aside.

Cut the cheese into cubes about 2.5 cm/1 inch square. Put the lettuce, tomatoes and cucumber in a salad bowl. Scatter over the cheese and toss together.

Just before serving, whisk the dressing, pour over the salad leaves and toss together. Scatter over the olives and chopped herbs and serve.

Salade Niçoise

Serves 4

- 2 tuna steaks, about 2 cm/¾ inch thick
- olive oil, for brushing
- 250 g/9 oz green beans, topped and tailed
- 125 ml/4 fl oz vinaigrette or garlic vinaigrette dressing
- 2 hearts of lettuce, leaves separated
- 3 large hard-boiled eggs, quartered
- 2 juicy vine-ripened tomatoes, cut into wedges
- 50 g/1¾ oz anchovy fillets in oil, drained
- 55 g/2 oz Niçoise olives, stoned
- salt and pepper

Heat a griddle pan over a high heat until you can feel the heat rising from the surface. Brush the tuna steaks with oil, place them oiled side down on the hot pan and chargrill for 2 minutes. Lightly brush the top side of the tuna steaks with more oil. Use a pair of tongs to turn over the steaks, then season to taste with salt and pepper. Continue chargrilling for a further 2 minutes for rare or up to 4 minutes for well done. Leave to cool.

Meanwhile, bring a saucepan of lightly salted water to the boil. Add the beans to the pan and return to the boil, then boil for 3 minutes, or until the beans are just tender. Drain the beans and immediately transfer them to a large bowl. Pour over the vinaigrette and stir together, then leave the beans to cool in the dressing.

To serve, line a platter with lettuce leaves. Lift the beans out of the bowl, leaving the excess dressing behind, and pile them in the centre of the platter. Break the tuna into large pieces and arrange it over the beans. Arrange the eggs and tomatoes around the side. Place the anchovy fillets over the salad, then scatter with the olives. Drizzle the remaining dressing over everything and serve.

Waldorf chicken salad

Serves 4

500 g/1 lb 2 oz red apples, diced

3 tbsp fresh lemon juice

150 ml/5 fl oz Mayonnaise (see page 24)

1 head celery

4 shallots, sliced

1 garlic clove, crushed

85 g/3 oz walnuts, chopped

500 g/1 lb 2 oz lean cooked chicken, cubed

1 cos lettuce

pepper

chopped walnuts, to garnish

Place the apples in a bowl with the lemon juice and 1 tablespoon of the mayonnaise. Set aside for 40 minutes or until required.

Slice the celery very thinly. Add the celery with the shallots, garlic and walnuts to the apple, mix and then add the remaining mayonnaise and blend thoroughly.

Add the chicken and mix with the other ingredients.

Line a serving dish with the lettuce. Pile the chicken salad into a serving bowl, sprinkle with pepper and garnish with the chopped walnuts.

Perfect roast potatoes

Serves 8

70 g/2½ oz goose or duck fat or 5 tbsp olive oil

1 kg/2 lb 4 oz even-sized potatoes, peeled

coarse sea salt

8 fresh rosemary sprigs, to garnish

Preheat the oven to 230°C/450°F/Gas Mark 8. Put the fat in a large roasting tin, sprinkle generously with sea salt and place in the oven.

Meanwhile, cook the potatoes in a large saucepan of boiling water for 8–10 minutes until par-boiled. Drain well and, if the potatoes are large, cut them in half. Return the potatoes to the empty saucepan and shake vigorously to roughen their outsides.

Arrange the potatoes in a single layer in the hot fat and roast for 45 minutes. If they look as if they are beginning to char around the edges, reduce the oven temperature to 200°C/400°F/Gas Mark 6. Turn the potatoes over and roast for a further 30 minutes until crisp. Serve garnished with rosemary sprigs.

Roasted vegetables

Serves 4

4 parsnips, scrubbed and trimmed but left unpeeled

4 carrots, scrubbed and trimmed but left unpeeled

2 onions, quartered

1 red onion, quartered

3 leeks, trimmed and cut into 6-cm/2½-inch slices

6 garlic cloves, left unpeeled and whole

6 tbsp extra virgin olive oil

½ tsp mild chilli powder

pinch of paprika

salt and pepper

Preheat the oven to 220°C/425°F/Gas Mark 7. Bring a large saucepan of water to the boil.

Cut the parsnips and carrots into wedges of similar size. Add them to the saucepan and cook for 5 minutes. Drain thoroughly and place in an ovenproof dish with the onions, leeks and garlic. Pour over the oil, sprinkle with the spices and salt and pepper to taste, then mix until all the vegetables are well coated.

Roast in the preheated oven for at least 1 hour. Turn the vegetables from time to time until they are tender and starting to colour. Remove from the oven, transfer to a warmed serving dish and serve immediately.

My special recipes

Notes

My special recipes

Notes

My special recipes

Notes

My special recipes

Notes

My special recipes

Notes

My special recipes

Notes

Pasta & grains

Making fresh pasta

For convenience, most of the recipes in this book use dried pasta. However, if you want to have a go at making filled pasta, such as ravioli, you will need to prepare the dough yourself. Making fresh pasta is not as difficult as you may believe and the same basic dough can also be used to make lasagne sheets and a variety of shapes, such as tagliatelle, pappardelle and macaroni. You won't need any special equipment (a pasta machine makes the job of rolling the dough simpler but it's not strictly necessary) and the process is both easy and satisfying.

Basic pasta dough

Serves 3–4

- 200 g/7 oz strong white bread flour, plus extra for dusting
- pinch of salt
- 2 eggs, lightly beaten
- 1 tbsp olive oil

Sift together the flour and salt onto a work surface and make a well in the centre with your fingers. Pour the eggs and oil into the well, then, using the fingers of one hand, gradually incorporate the flour into the liquid. Knead the dough on a lightly floured work surface until it is completely smooth.

Wrap in clingfilm and leave to rest for 30 minutes before rolling out or feeding through a pasta machine.

Flavoured pasta

The Basic Pasta Dough recipe may be flavoured and coloured by the addition of other ingredients.

Tomato pasta: Add 2 tablespoons of tomato purée to the well in the flour and use only 1½ eggs instead of 2.

Herb pasta: Add 3 tablespoons of finely chopped fresh herbs to the flour before making a well and adding the eggs and oil.

Spinach pasta: Blanch 225 g/8 oz spinach leaves in boiling water for 1 minute. Squeeze out the excess water, finely chop and add to the flour before making a well and adding the eggs and oil.

Wholemeal pasta: Use 140 g/5 oz wholemeal flour with 25 g/1 oz strong white bread flour.

Rolling out pasta dough

When the dough has rested, it may be rolled out. Large quantities of dough should be halved or cut into quarters before rolling out. Keep covered until you are ready to work on them. To roll out by hand, lightly dust a work surface with plain flour, then roll out the pasta dough with a lightly floured rolling pin, always rolling away from you and turning the dough a quarter turn each time. Keep rolling to make a rectangle 2–3 mm/1⁄16–1⁄8 inch thick. The dough can then be cut into ribbons, stamped out with a biscuit cutter or filled and cut out to make ravioli.

A pasta machine makes rolling out the dough easier and quicker and ensures that it is even. There are a number of models available, the most useful being a hand-cranked machine with attachable cutters. An electric machine is even easier to use but somewhat extravagant.

Cut the dough into manageable-sized pieces – 1 quantity Basic Pasta Dough should be cut into 4 pieces, for example. Flatten a piece with your hand and wrap the other pieces in clingfilm until required. Fold the flat piece of dough into thirds and feed it through the pasta machine on its widest setting. Repeat the folding and rolling 3 or 4 more times on this setting, then close the rollers by one notch. Continue feeding the dough through the rollers, without folding into thirds, gradually reducing the setting until you reach the narrowest. If you want to make ribbons, cut the dough into 30-cm/12-inch strips and feed through the appropriate cutter.

Pasta sauces

Tomato Sauce

Serves 4

- 2 tbsp olive oil
- 1 small onion, chopped
- 1 garlic clove, finely chopped
- 400 g/14 oz canned chopped tomatoes
- 2 tbsp chopped fresh flat-leaf parsley
- 1 tsp dried oregano
- 2 bay leaves
- 2 tbsp tomato purée
- 1 tsp sugar
- salt and pepper

Heat the oil in a saucepan. Add the onion and garlic and cook over a low heat, stirring occasionally, for 5 minutes until soft.

Increase the heat to medium, stir in the tomatoes, parsley, oregano, bay leaves, tomato purée and sugar, and season to taste with salt and pepper.

Bring to the boil, then reduce the heat and simmer, uncovered, for 15–20 minutes until reduced by half. Taste and adjust the seasoning, if necessary, and remove and discard the bay leaves.

Italian Cheese Sauce

Serves 4–6

- 55 g/2 oz butter
- 25 g/1 oz plain flour
- 300 ml/10 fl oz hot milk
- pinch of ground nutmeg
- pinch of dried thyme
- 2 tbsp white wine vinegar
- 3 tbsp double cream
- 55 g/2 oz grated mozzarella cheese
- 55 g/2 oz grated Parmesan cheese
- 1 tsp English mustard
- 2 tbsp soured cream
- salt and pepper

Melt the butter in a saucepan and stir in the flour. Cook, stirring, over a low heat until the mixture is light in colour and crumbly in texture. Stir in the hot milk and cook, stirring, for 15 minutes until thick and smooth.

Add the nutmeg, thyme and vinegar and season to taste. Stir in the cream and mix well.

Stir in the cheeses, mustard and soured cream and mix until the cheeses have melted and blended into the sauce.

Pesto

Serves 4

- 2 handfuls fresh basil leaves
- 50 g/1¾ oz pine kernels
- 1 garlic clove, coarsely chopped
- 50 g/1¾ oz freshly grated Parmesan cheese
- 6–8 tbsp extra virgin olive oil
- salt

Put the basil, pine kernels and garlic in a mortar. Add a pinch of salt and pound to a paste with a pestle.

Transfer the mixture to a bowl and gradually work in the Parmesan cheese with a wooden spoon. Gradually stir in the olive oil until the sauce is thick and creamy. Cover with clingfilm and store in the refrigerator until ready to use.

Spaghetti bolognese

Serves 4

1 tbsp olive oil

1 onion, finely chopped

2 garlic cloves, chopped

1 carrot, chopped

1 celery stick, chopped

50 g/1¾ oz pancetta or streaky bacon, diced

350 g/12 oz fresh lean beef mince

400 g/14 oz canned chopped tomatoes

2 tsp dried oregano

125 ml/4 fl oz red wine

2 tbsp tomato purée

350 g/12 oz dried spaghetti

salt and pepper

chopped fresh parsley, to garnish

Heat the oil in a large frying pan. Add the onion and cook for 3 minutes. Add the garlic, carrot, celery and pancetta and sauté for 3–4 minutes, or until just beginning to brown.

Add the beef and cook over a high heat for another 3 minutes or until all of the meat is browned. Stir in the tomatoes, oregano and red wine and bring to the boil. Reduce the heat and leave to simmer for about 45 minutes.

Stir in the tomato purée and season to taste with salt and pepper.

Bring a large, heavy-based saucepan of lightly salted water to the boil. Add the spaghetti, return to the boil and cook for 8–10 minutes until the pasta is tender but still firm to the bite. Drain thoroughly.

Transfer the spaghetti to a serving plate and pour over the sauce. Toss to mix well, garnish with parsley and serve hot.

Tagliatelle alla carbonara

Serves 4

- 450 g/1 lb dried tagliatelle
- 1 tbsp olive oil
- 225 g/8 oz rindless pancetta or streaky bacon, chopped
- 4 eggs
- 5 tbsp single cream
- 2 tbsp freshly grated Parmesan cheese
- salt and pepper

Bring a large, heavy-based saucepan of lightly salted water to the boil. Add the pasta, return to the boil and cook for 8–10 minutes, or until the pasta is tender but still firm to the bite.

Meanwhile, heat the oil in a heavy-based frying pan. Add the pancetta and cook over a medium heat, stirring frequently, for 8–10 minutes.

Beat the eggs with the cream in a small bowl and season to taste with salt and pepper. Drain the pasta and return it to the pan. Tip in the contents of the frying pan, then add the egg mixture and half the Parmesan cheese. Stir well, then transfer to a warmed serving dish. Serve immediately, sprinkled with the remaining cheese.

Spinach & ricotta ravioli

Serves 4

350 g/12 oz spinach leaves, coarse stalks removed

225 g/8 oz ricotta cheese

55 g/2 oz freshly grated Parmesan cheese, plus extra to serve

2 eggs

pinch of freshly grated nutmeg

pepper

1 quantity Spinach Pasta Dough (see page 60)

plain flour, for dusting

To make the filling, place the spinach in a heavy-based saucepan with just the water clinging to the leaves after washing, then cover and cook over a low heat for 5 minutes, or until wilted. Drain well and squeeze out as much moisture as possible. Leave to cool, then chop finely.

Beat the ricotta cheese until smooth, then stir in the spinach, Parmesan cheese and 1 egg and season to taste with nutmeg and pepper.

Divide the dough in half and wrap 1 piece in clingfilm. Roll out the other piece on a lightly floured surface to a rectangle 2–3 mm/$^{1}/_{16}$–$^{1}/_{8}$ inch thick. Cover with a damp tea towel and roll out the other piece of dough to the same size. Place teaspoonfuls of the filling in rows 4 cm/1$^{1}/_{2}$ inches apart on a sheet of dough. In a small bowl, lightly beat the remaining egg and use to brush the spaces between the mounds. Place the second sheet of dough on top of the first and press down firmly between the pockets of filling, pushing out any air bubbles. Cut into squares with a sharp knife. Place on a floured tea towel and leave to stand for 1 hour.

Bring a large, heavy-based saucepan of lightly salted water to the boil, add the ravioli, in batches, return to the boil and cook for 5 minutes. Remove with a slotted spoon and drain on kitchen paper. Transfer to a warmed serving dish and serve immediately, sprinkled with Parmesan cheese.

Beef lasagne with ricotta cheese

Serves 6

175 ml/6 fl oz olive oil

55 g/2 oz butter, plus extra for greasing

85 g/3 oz bacon or pancetta, diced

1 onion, finely chopped

1 celery stick, finely chopped

1 carrot, finely chopped

350 g/12 oz beef topside in a single piece

5 tbsp red wine

2 tbsp sun-dried tomato purée

200 g/7 oz Italian sausage, such as luganega

2 eggs

115 g/4 oz Parmesan cheese, freshly grated

25 g/1 oz fresh breadcrumbs

350 g/12 oz ricotta cheese

8 sheets no pre-cook lasagne

350 g/12 oz mozzarella cheese, sliced

salt and pepper

chopped fresh parsley, to garnish

Heat 100 ml/3½ fl oz of the oil with the butter in a large saucepan. Add the bacon, onion, celery and carrot and cook over a low heat, stirring occasionally, for 5 minutes until soft. Increase the heat to medium, add the beef and cook, turning occasionally, until evenly browned. Stir in the red wine and tomato purée, season and bring just to the boil. Reduce the heat, cover and simmer gently, for 1½ hours until the beef is tender.

Meanwhile, heat 2 tablespoons of the remaining oil in a frying pan. Add the sausage and cook, turning frequently, for 8–10 minutes. Remove the sausage from the pan, remove the skin, thinly slice the meat and set aside. Transfer the beef to a chopping board and dice finely. Return half the beef to the sauce. Mix the remaining beef with 1 egg, 1 tablespoon of Parmesan cheese and the breadcrumbs in a bowl and shape into walnut-sized balls. Heat the remaining oil in a frying pan. Cook the meatballs, turning frequently, for 5–8 minutes. Remove with a slotted spoon and set aside.

Pass the ricotta through a sieve into a bowl. Stir in the remaining egg and 4 tablespoons of the Parmesan cheese and season. Preheat the oven to 180°C/350°F/Gas Mark 4. Grease a rectangular ovenproof dish with butter. Make layers of lasagne sheets, ricotta mixture, meat sauce, meatballs, sausage and mozzarella cheese in the prepared dish. Finish with a layer of the ricotta mixture and sprinkle with the remaining Parmesan cheese. Bake for 20–25 minutes, or until golden brown. Remove from the oven, garnish with parsley and serve.

Chilli con carne

Serves 4

750 g/1 lb 10 oz lean stewing steak
2 tbsp vegetable oil
1 large onion, sliced
2–4 garlic cloves, crushed
1 tbsp plain flour
425 ml/15 fl oz tomato juice
400 g/14 oz canned tomatoes
1–2 tbsp sweet chilli sauce
1 tsp ground cumin
425 g/15 oz canned red kidney beans, drained and rinsed
½ teaspoon dried oregano
1–2 tbsp chopped fresh parsley
salt and pepper
sprigs of fresh herbs, to garnish
freshly cooked rice and tortillas, to serve

Preheat the oven to 160°C/325°F/Gas Mark 3. Using a sharp knife, cut the beef into 2-cm/¾-inch cubes. Heat the vegetable oil in a large flameproof casserole dish and fry the beef over a medium heat until well sealed on all sides. Remove the beef from the casserole with a slotted spoon and reserve until required.

Add the onion and garlic to the casserole and fry until lightly browned, then stir in the flour and cook for 1–2 minutes.

Stir in the tomato juice and tomatoes and bring to the boil. Return the beef to the casserole and add the chilli sauce, cumin and salt and pepper to taste. Cover and cook in the preheated oven for 1½ hours, or until the beef is almost tender.

Stir in the kidney beans, oregano and parsley, and adjust the seasoning to taste, if necessary. Cover the casserole and return to the oven for 45 minutes. Transfer to 4 large, warmed serving plates, garnish with sprigs of fresh herbs and serve immediately with freshly cooked rice and tortillas.

Parmesan cheese risotto with mushrooms

serves 4

- 1 litre/1¾ pints Vegetable Stock (see page 20)
- 2 tbsp olive oil or vegetable oil
- 225 g/8 oz risotto rice
- 2 garlic cloves, crushed
- 1 onion, chopped
- 2 celery sticks, chopped
- 1 red or green pepper, deseeded and chopped
- 225 g/8 oz mushrooms, thinly sliced
- 1 tbsp chopped fresh oregano or 1 tsp dried oregano
- 55 g/2 oz sun-dried tomatoes in olive oil, drained and chopped (optional)
- 55 g/2 oz finely grated Parmesan cheese
- salt and pepper
- chopped fresh flat-leaf parsley, to garnish

Bring the stock to the boil in a saucepan, then reduce the heat and keep simmering gently over a low heat while you are cooking the risotto.

Heat the oil in a deep saucepan. Add the rice and cook over a low heat, stirring constantly, for 2–3 minutes until the grains are thoroughly coated in oil and translucent.

Add the garlic, onion, celery and pepper and cook, stirring frequently, for 5 minutes. Add the mushrooms and cook for 3–4 minutes. Stir in the oregano.

Gradually add the hot stock, a ladleful at a time. Stir constantly and add more liquid as the rice absorbs each addition. Increase the heat to medium so that the liquid bubbles. Cook for 20 minutes, or until all the liquid has been absorbed and the rice is creamy. Add the sun-dried tomatoes, if using, 5 minutes before the end of the cooking time and season to taste with salt and pepper.

Remove the risotto from the heat and stir in half the cheese until it melts. Transfer the risotto to warmed plates. Top with the remaining cheese, garnish with the parsley and serve immediately.

My special recipes

Notes

My special recipes

Notes

My special recipes

Notes

My special recipes

Notes

My special recipes

Notes

My special recipes

Notes

Meat

Choosing meat

Terms applied to different varieties of a particular meat, such as lamb, are often related to the age of the animal. The meat of younger animals is generally more tender, but also less pronounced in flavour, while the meat of older animals is likely to be tougher yet tastier.

Beef and veal

Beef is the meat provided by domestic cattle, while veal is the meat of the young calf. Beef usually comes from castrated male cattle slaughtered at between 18 and 24 months, and veal from male calves slaughtered at either 3 weeks, 18–20 weeks or 5–6 months. There are many types of beef produced from a large number of different types of cattle, including: 'dairy cross' meat from the offspring of a dairy cow and a bull, 'prime beef' from a pedigree herd, 'rare' beef from breeds such as Aberdeen Angus, or prized 'kobe beef', which comes from Wagyu cattle.

Lamb and Mutton

Lamb is the meat from a young sheep, and there are several types.
Baby lamb/suckling: milk-fed lamb no older than 10 weeks and weighing less than 9.1 kg/20 lb.
Spring lamb: several months old and 9.1–18 kg/20–40 lb.
Lamb: 5–12 months, and most commonly available.
Hogget/yearling: meat from a lamb that is 1–2 years old.
Mutton: meat of a mature sheep over 2 years old.

Pork, ham and bacon

Pork is the fresh meat of the domesticated pig. Traditionally, pork was seasonal meat, much of which was salted and preserved to provide ham, bacon and sausages. Most pork is slaughtered at 6–9 months, and anything older is termed a 'hog'. 'Rare-breed' pork is almost exclusively free-range.

Offal

The term 'offal' derives from 'off-all' and refers to the edible parts of an animal left when the meat is removed from the carcass. This includes organs such as heart, liver and kidneys as well as tongue, brain, thymus gland (sweetbreads), stomach lining (tripe) and blood (used in black or blood pudding). Offal also covers pig's feet/trotters, head and cheek, ox tail and calf's foot.

Cooking times & temperatures

Thorough cooking of meat is very important, particularly in the case of pork, which can carry harmful bacteria and cause food poisoning if not cooked all the way through. It's essential to set the oven to the correct temperature and cook for the time recommended for the weight of the piece of meat. A meat thermometer is a useful device for testing whether a joint of meat is cooked thoroughly. Simply insert the thermometer into the thickest part of the meat at the start of cooking, taking care to avoid contact with any bone, which might produce a false reading. When the thermometer reaches the required temperature, the meat is cooked.

Beef

Preheat the oven to 230°C/450°F/Gas Mark 8.
Roast for 20 minutes, then reduce the temperature to 190°C/375°F/Gas Mark 5 and roast for:

- 15 minutes per 450 g/1 lb for rare
- 20 minutes per 450 g/1 lb for medium
- 30 minutes per 450 g/1 lb for well done.

Meat thermometer recommended internal temperature:
Rare: 60°C/140°F
Medium: 71°C/160°F
Well done: 76°C/169°F

Lamb

Preheat the oven to 190°C/375°F/Gas Mark 5.

Roast for 30 minutes per 450 g/1 lb, 30 minutes less for rare.

Meat thermometer recommended internal temperature: 82°C/180°F

Pork

Preheat the oven to 230°C/450°F/Gas Mark 8:

Roast for 25 minutes, then reduce the temperature to 190°C/375°F/Gas Mark 5 and roast for 35 minutes per 450 g/1 lb.

Meat thermometer recommended internal temperature:
Pork: 87°C/189°F
Bacon/gammon joint: 71°C/160°F

Roast beef

Serves 8

1 prime rib of beef, weighing 2.7 kg/6 lb

2 tsp English mustard powder

1 tbsp plain flour

red wine (optional)

salt and pepper

Beef Gravy and Quick Horseradish Sauce (see page 79), to serve

Preheat the oven to 230°C/450°F/Gas Mark 8. Season the meat to taste with salt and pepper and rub in the mustard and the flour.

Put the meat in a roasting tin large enough to hold it comfortably and roast in the preheated oven for 15 minutes. Reduce the heat to 190°C/375°F/Gas Mark 5 and cook for 1 hour 45 minutes for rare beef or 2 hours 20 minutes for medium beef. Baste the meat occasionally to keep it moist. If the tin becomes too dry, add a little red wine.

When the meat is cooked, transfer to a warmed serving plate, cover loosely with foil and leave to rest for 10–15 minutes.

When ready to serve, carve the meat into slices and serve on warmed plates. Serve with the Beef Gravy in a warmed jug, and with some Quick Horseradish Sauce on the side.

Quick horseradish sauce

Serves 8

6 tbsp creamed horseradish sauce

6 tbsp crème fraîche

Mix the horseradish and crème fraîche together in a small bowl until well blended.

Serve the sauce with roast beef.

Beef gravy

Serves 8

pan juices from a meat roasting tin

2 tbsp flour

300 ml/10 fl oz red wine

300 ml/10 fl oz Beef Stock (see page 21)

Worcestershire sauce (optional)

salt and pepper

Pour off most of the fat from the roasting tin, leaving behind the meat juices and the sediment. Put the roasting tin over a medium heat and scrape all the sediment from the base of the tin. Sprinkle in the flour and quickly mix it into the juices with a small whisk. When you have a smooth paste, gradually add the wine and most of the stock, whisking constantly. Bring to the boil, then reduce the heat to a gentle simmer and cook for 2–3 minutes. Season to taste with salt and pepper and add the remaining stock, if necessary, and a little Worcestershire sauce, if using.

Roast pork

Serves 4

1 boned pork loin joint, weighing 1 kg/2 lb 4 oz, rind removed and reserved

2 tbsp mustard

salt and pepper

Apple sauce

450 g/1 lb Bramley apples, peeled, cored and sliced

3 tablespoons water

15 g/½ oz caster sugar

pinch of ground cinnamon (optional)

15 g/½ oz butter (optional)

Gravy

1 tbsp flour

300 ml/10 fl oz cider, apple juice or Chicken Stock (see page 21)

salt and pepper

Preheat the oven to 200°C/400°F/Gas Mark 6. Score the pork rind with a sharp knife and sprinkle with salt. Put it on a wire rack set over a baking tray and roast in the preheated oven for 30–40 minutes until the crackling is golden and crisp.

Season the pork well with salt and pepper and spread the fat with the mustard. Put in a roasting tin and roast in the centre of the oven for 20 minutes. Reduce the temperature to 190°C/375°F/Gas Mark 5 and cook for a further 50–60 minutes until the meat is well browned and the juices run clear when a skewer is inserted into the thickest part of the meat. Remove the meat from the oven and transfer to a warmed serving plate, cover loosely with foil and leave in a warm place to rest.

Meanwhile, to make the sauce, put all the ingredients into a saucepan over a low heat. Cook for 10 minutes, stirring occasionally. Beat well until the sauce is thick and smooth – use a hand-held electric whisk for a smooth finish.

To make the gravy, pour off most of the fat from the roasting tin. Place the tin over a medium heat and scrape the sediment from the base of the tin. Sprinkle in the flour and quickly whisk it into the juices. When you have a smooth paste, gradually add the cider, whisking constantly. Bring to the boil, then reduce the heat and simmer for 2–3 minutes until thick. Season with salt and pepper, pour into a warmed serving jug and serve with the pork, with some Apple Sauce on the side.

Roast lamb

Serves 6

1 leg of lamb, weighing 1.5 kg/3 lb 5 oz

6 garlic cloves, thinly sliced lengthways

8 fresh rosemary sprigs

4 tbsp olive oil

salt and pepper

Redcurrant glaze

4 tbsp redcurrant jelly

300 ml/10 fl oz rosé wine

Preheat the oven to 200°C/400°F/Gas Mark 6. Using a small, sharp knife, cut slits all over the leg of lamb. Insert 1–2 garlic slices and 4–5 rosemary needles into each slit. Put any remaining rosemary in the base of a roasting tin. Season the lamb to taste with salt and pepper and put in the roasting tin. Pour over the oil. Cover with foil and roast in the preheated oven for 1 hour 20 minutes.

To make the glaze, mix the redcurrant jelly and wine together in a small saucepan. Heat over a low heat, stirring constantly, until combined. Bring to the boil, then reduce the heat and simmer until reduced. Remove the lamb from the oven and pour over the glaze. Return to the oven and roast, uncovered, for about 10 minutes, depending on how well done you like it.

Remove the lamb from the roasting tin and transfer to a carving board. Cover loosely with foil and leave to rest for 15 minutes before carving and serving.

The classic hamburger

Serves 4–6

450 g/1 lb rump steak or topside, freshly minced

1 onion, grated

2–4 garlic cloves, crushed

2 tsp wholegrain mustard

2 tbsp olive oil

450 g/1 lb onions, finely sliced

2 tsp light muscovado sugar

pepper

hamburger buns, to serve

Place the minced steak, grated onion, garlic, mustard and pepper in a large bowl and mix together. Shape into 4–6 equal-sized burgers, then cover and set aside to chill for 30 minutes.

Meanwhile, heat the oil in a heavy-based frying pan. Add the sliced onions and sauté over a low heat for 10–15 minutes, or until the onions have caramelized. Add the sugar after 8 minutes and stir occasionally during cooking. Drain well on kitchen paper and keep warm.

Preheat the grill. Cook the burgers for 3–5 minutes on each side, or until cooked to personal preference. Serve in hamburger buns with the onions.

Peppered T-bone steak

Serves 2

2 tbsp whole black peppercorns, green peppercorns, or a mixture of both

2 T-bone steaks, about 250 g/9 oz each

2 tbsp butter

1 tbsp olive or sunflower oil

125 ml/4 fl oz red wine

salt

freshly cooked vegetables and cooked rice, to serve

Put the peppercorns into a mortar and coarsely crush with a pestle, or put into a strong polythene bag, place on a chopping board and coarsely crush with the end of a rolling pin.

Spread out the crushed peppercorns on a plate and firmly press one side of each steak into them to encrust the surface of the meat. Turn over and repeat with the other side.

Melt the butter with the oil in a large, heavy-based frying pan over a high heat. When hot, add the steaks and cook quickly on both sides to seal. Reduce the heat to medium and cook, turning once, for 2½–3 minutes each side for rare, 3½–5 minutes each side for medium, or 5–7 minutes each side for well done. Transfer the steaks to warmed plates and keep warm.

Add the wine to the pan and stir to deglaze by scraping any sediment from the bottom of the pan. Bring to the boil and boil until reduced by about half. Season to taste with salt. Pour the pan juices over the steaks and serve at once with freshly cooked vegetables and rice.

My special recipes

Notes

My special recipes

Notes

My special recipes

Notes

My special recipes

Notes

My special recipes

Notes

My special recipes

Notes

Poultry

Choosing poultry

Poultry is defined as domestic fowl bred specifically for eating. Raised for their meat and eggs, poultry includes chicken, turkey, duck, goose and guinea fowl.

Chicken

Chicken is the most popular and widely available form of poultry. It is sold under a number of different names according to its age, size and method of rearing. The following are the most common types of chicken:
Poussin: an immature chicken, 4–6 weeks old, weighing up to 450 g/1 lb, with delicate, moist meat.
Spring chicken: a small, young bird weighing up to 1.15 kg/2 lb 8 oz.
Broiler or roasting chicken: the most common bird for roasting, a full-sized bird weighs 1.3–2.7 kg/3–6 lb.
Boiling fowl: an older bird, usually a laying hen weighing 2.7 kg/6 lb.
Capon: a castrated young chicken bred for its tender, white flesh.
Corn fed: chicken fed on corn, which produces a yellow flesh and skin with a flavour comparable to guinea fowl.
Free range: indicates that a limited number of birds are housed per square metre/yard and have outside access for at least half their life.
Traditional free range: indicates chickens that have more space and must have had outside access from the age of 6 weeks.
Free range–total freedom: this is very similar to traditional free range, except that during daylight hours, they have unrestricted outside access.
Battery: intensively reared chickens with no outside access, slaughtered at 6 weeks.
Organic: chickens raised according to a strictly regulated standard of welfare. They are GM-free and have been fed with antibiotic-free food, with guaranteed access to forage and feed outside.

Turkey

Descended from the North American wild turkey, this domesticated bird is available all year round. A young turkey weighing 3.6–11 kg/8–24 lb will provide about 70 per cent white meat and 30 per cent dark meat. Allow an average of 350 g/12 oz per person. The rearing methods for turkeys are similar to chickens, so an organic, free-range bird will have a better flavour and texture than an intensively raised bird.

Duck

Duck is a waterfowl, now mainly raised commercially and widely available. There are a number of varieties, and as with all poultry, a younger, free-range bird will taste better than an older, farmed bird. Most ducks on offer is duckling, which is 6–8 weeks old, but ducks up to 16 weeks old is sometimes sold. A 2.7-kg/6-lb duck will feed 2–3 people.

Goose

Goose is a large water bird popular for roasting and raised free range. Fatty and with rich meat, it has an average weight of 2.7–5.4 kg/6–12 lb, but because of its meat to fat ratio, a goose will feed only four people, on average.

Cooking times & temperatures

It is essential to cook poultry all the way through in order to kill off any potentially harmful bacteria. It is important to remember that individual oven temperatures and cooking times vary, so the recommended cooking times are only ever approximate. You can check whether a bird is cooked by inserting a sharp knife or skewer into the thickest part; if the juices run clear, it is cooked. If not, return it to the oven and cook until done. Alternatively, you can insert a meat thermometer into the thickest part of the bird at the start of cooking, avoiding contact with any bone, which may produce a false reading. The bird is cooked when the temperature reaches 90°C/194°F.

Chicken

Preheat the oven to 190°C/375°F/Gas Mark 5.

Roast for 20 minutes per 450 g/1 lb, plus 20 minutes. Increase the temperature to 220°C/425°F/Gas Mark 7 for the final 15 minutes of the calculated time.

Turkey

Preheat the oven to 220°C/425°F/Gas Mark 7.
For turkeys weighing 3.5–4.5 kg/8–10 lb, roast for 30 minutes, then reduce the temperature to 160°C/325°F/Gas Mark 3 for 2½–3 hours, increasing the temperature to 200°C/400°F/Gas Mark 6, uncovered, for the final 30 minutes.
For turkeys weighing 5.5–6.5 kg/12–14 lb, roast for 40 minutes, then reduce the temperature to 160°C/325°F/Gas Mark 3 for 3–3½ hours, increasing the temperature to 200°C/400°F/Gas Mark 6, uncovered, for the final 30 minutes.

Duck

Preheat the oven to 220°C/425°F/Gas Mark 7.

Roast for 20 minutes, then reduce the temperature to 180°C/350°F/Gas Mark 4 and roast for 1 hour–1 hour 10 minutes.

Goose

Preheat the oven to 220°C/425°F/Gas Mark 7.

Roast for 20 minutes, then reduce the temperature to 180°C/350°F/Gas Mark 4 and roast for 1 hour 20 minutes–2 hours.

Traditional roast chicken

Serves 6

1 x 2.25-kg/5-lb free-range chicken
55 g/2 oz butter
2 tbsp chopped fresh lemon thyme
1 lemon, quartered
125 ml/4 fl oz white wine
salt and pepper
6 fresh thyme sprigs, to garnish

Preheat the oven to 220°C/425°F/Gas Mark 7. Make sure the chicken is clean, wiping it inside and out with kitchen paper, and place in a roasting tin. In a bowl, soften the butter with a fork, mix in the thyme and season well with salt and pepper. Butter the chicken all over with the herb butter, inside and out, and place the lemon pieces inside the body cavity. Pour the wine over the chicken.

Roast in the centre of the preheated oven for 20 minutes. Reduce the temperature to 190°C/375°F/Gas Mark 5 and roast for a further 1¼ hours, basting frequently. Cover with foil if the skin begins to brown too much. If the tin dries out, add a little more wine or water.

Test that the chicken is cooked by piercing the thickest part of the leg with a sharp knife or skewer and making sure the juices run clear. Remove from the oven. Transfer the chicken to a warmed serving plate, cover loosely with foil and leave to rest for 10 minutes before carving. Place the roasting tin on the hob and bubble the juices gently over a low heat until they have reduced and are thick and glossy. Season to taste with salt and pepper. Serve the chicken with the juices and scatter with the thyme sprigs.

Boned & stuffed roast duck

Serves 6–8

1.8 kg/4 lb duck (dressed weight); ask your butcher to bone the duck and cut off the wings at the first joint

450 g/1 lb flavoured sausage meat, such as pork and apricot

1 small onion, finely chopped

1 Cox's apple, cored and finely chopped

85 g/3 oz dried apricots, finely chopped

85 g/3 oz chopped walnuts

2 tbsp chopped fresh parsley

1 large or 2 smaller duck breasts, skin removed

salt and pepper

Apricot sauce

400 g/14 oz canned apricot halves, in syrup

150 ml/5 fl oz Chicken Stock (see page 21)

125 ml/4 fl oz Marsala

½ tbsp ground cinnamon

½ tbsp ground ginger

salt and pepper

Preheat the oven to 190°C/375°F/Gas Mark 5. Wipe the duck with kitchen paper both inside and out. Lay it, skin side down on a board and season well with salt and pepper.

Mix together the sausage meat, onion, apple, apricots, walnuts and parsley and season well with salt and pepper. Form into a large sausage shape.

Lay the duck breast(s) on the whole duck and cover with the stuffing. Wrap the whole duck around the filling and tuck in any leg and neck flaps. Sew the duck up the back and across both ends with fine string. Try to use one piece of string so that you can remove it in one go. Mould the duck into a good shape and place, sewn side down, on a wire rack over a roasting tin. Roast for 1½–2 hours, basting occasionally. When it is cooked, the duck should be golden brown and crispy.

Meanwhile, make the sauce. Whiz the apricot halves with their syrup in a blender until a purée forms. Pour the purée into a saucepan and add the stock, Marsala, cinnamon and ginger and season to taste with salt and pepper. Stir over a low heat, then simmer for 2–3 minutes.

Carve the duck into thick slices at the table and serve with the warm apricot sauce.

Roast turkey

Serves 8

1 quantity ready-made stuffing

1 x 5-kg/11-lb turkey

40 g/1½ oz butter

Bread Sauce (see page 97) and Cranberry Sauce (see page 97), to serve

Preheat the oven to 220°C/425°F/Gas Mark 7. Spoon the stuffing into the neck cavity of the turkey and close the flap of skin with a skewer. Place the bird in a large roasting tin and rub it all over with the butter. Roast in the preheated oven for 1 hour, then reduce the oven temperature to 180°C/350°F/Gas Mark 4 and roast for a further 2½ hours. You may need to pour off the fat from the roasting tin occasionally.

Check that the turkey is cooked by inserting a skewer or the point of a sharp knife into the thigh – if the juices run clear, it is ready. Transfer the bird to a carving board, cover loosely with foil and leave to rest.

Carve the turkey and serve with warm Bread Sauce and Cranberry Sauce.

Bread sauce

Serves 8

1 onion, peeled

4 cloves

600 ml/1 pint milk

115 g/4 oz fresh white breadcrumbs

55 g/2 oz butter

salt and pepper

Stud the onion with the cloves, then place in a saucepan with the milk, breadcrumbs and butter. Bring just to boiling point over a low heat, then remove from the heat and leave to stand in a warm place to infuse. Just before serving, remove the onion and cloves and reheat the sauce gently, beating well with a wooden spoon. Season to taste with salt and pepper.

Cranberry sauce

Serves 8

thinly pared rind and juice of 1 lemon

thinly pared rind and juice of 1 orange

350 g/12 oz cranberries, thawed, if frozen

140 g/5 oz caster sugar

2 tbsp arrowroot, mixed with 3 tbsp cold water

Cut the strips of lemon and orange rind into thin shreds and place in a heavy-based saucepan. If using fresh cranberries, rinse well and remove any stalks. Add the berries, citrus juice and sugar to the saucepan and cook over a medium heat, stirring occasionally, for 5 minutes, or until the berries begin to burst.

Strain the juice into a clean saucepan and reserve the cranberries. Stir the arrowroot mixture into the juice, then bring to the boil, stirring constantly, until the sauce is smooth and thickened. Remove from the heat and stir in the reserved cranberries.

Transfer the cranberry sauce to a bowl and leave to cool, then cover with clingfilm and chill in the refrigerator.

Chicken fajitas

Serves 4

4 skinless, boneless chicken breasts

2 red peppers, deseeded and cut into 2.5-cm/1-inch strips

8 flour tortillas, warmed

Marinade

3 tbsp olive oil, plus extra for drizzling

3 tbsp maple syrup or honey

1 tbsp red wine vinegar

2 garlic cloves, crushed

2 tsp dried oregano

1–2 tsp dried red pepper flakes

salt and pepper

To serve

guacamole

soured cream

bottled salsa

shredded Webbs lettuce

To make the marinade, place the oil, maple syrup, vinegar, garlic, oregano, pepper flakes, and salt and pepper to taste in a large, shallow dish or bowl and mix together.

Slice the chicken across the grain into slices 2.5 cm/1 inch thick. Toss in the marinade until well coated. Cover and leave to chill in the refrigerator for 2–3 hours, turning occasionally.

Heat a griddle pan until hot. Lift the chicken slices from the marinade with a slotted spoon, lay them on the pan and cook over a medium–high heat for 3–4 minutes on each side until cooked through. Transfer the chicken to a warmed serving plate and keep warm.

Add the peppers, skin side down, to the pan and cook for 2 minutes on each side. Transfer to the serving plate.

Pile the cooked chicken and peppers onto the warmed tortillas, along with some guacamole, soured cream, salsa and shredded lettuce.

Italian turkey steaks

Serves 4

1 tbsp olive oil

4 turkey escalopes or steaks

2 red peppers, deseeded and sliced

1 red onion, sliced

2 garlic cloves, finely chopped

300 ml/10 fl oz passata

150 ml/5 fl oz medium white wine

1 tbsp chopped fresh marjoram

400 g/14 oz canned cannellini beans, drained and rinsed

3 tbsp fresh white breadcrumbs

salt and pepper

fresh basil sprigs, to garnish

Preheat the grill to medium. Heat the oil in a flameproof casserole or heavy-based frying pan. Add the turkey escalopes and cook over a medium heat for 5–10 minutes, turning occasionally, until golden. Transfer to a warmed plate.

Add the red peppers and onion to the frying pan and cook over a low heat, stirring occasionally, for 5 minutes, or until soft. Add the garlic and cook for a further 2 minutes.

Return the turkey to the frying pan and add the passata, wine and marjoram. Season to taste with salt and pepper. Bring to the boil, then reduce the heat, cover and simmer, stirring occasionally, for 25–30 minutes, or until the turkey is cooked through and tender.

Stir in the cannellini beans and simmer for a further 5 minutes. Sprinkle the breadcrumbs over the top and place under the preheated grill for 2–3 minutes, or until golden. Serve, garnished with fresh basil sprigs.

My special recipes

Notes

My special recipes

Notes

My special recipes

Notes

My special recipes

Notes

My special recipes

Notes

My special recipes

Notes

Fish & seafood

Buying and storing fish & shellfish

Buying

Freshness is the all-important factor to consider when buying any seafood that hasn't been preserved. Fresh fish is highly perishable so, unless you have access to supplies as they are landed, much of the 'fresh' fish on offer will have been frozen on the fishing vessel and then thawed. It is vitally important for you to know the signs of fish in prime condition and those specimens that you should avoid.

Whether you are buying your seafood at a supermarket's fish counter, from a fishmonger or from a market stall, the display slab should be spotlessly clean and there should be plenty of crushed ice around the seafood. Whole, gutted fish deteriorate less quickly than steaks or fillets, so look for a display that includes these.

Good-quality fish has a fresh, ocean-like aroma. It shouldn't smell 'fishy'. If there is any whiff of ammonia or unpleasantness, don't buy. Whole fish should be firm, not floppy, and the flesh should feel firm and elastic when you press gently. The eyes should be protruding and clear, not sunken or cloudy; any scales should be shiny and tight against the skin; the gills should be clear and bright red, not dull or grey. Fillets and steaks should be cleanly cut and look moist and fresh, with a shiny 'bloom' on the surface and no yellowing or browning.

Never buy packaged fish with damaged packaging. There should not be much air between the fish and the wrapping or any pools of liquid or blood. And, of course, you should always check the use-by date.

The term 'shellfish' includes bivalves (clams, mussels, oysters, scallops), crustaceans (crabs, lobsters, prawns) and cephalopods (squid and octopus). They should all be consumed on the day of purchase.

When clams, mussels and oysters are sold alive, the shells should be tightly closed; if open shells don't snap shut when tapped, they are dead. They should be in a net or porous bag (not a polythene bag). Most scallops are sold shucked, often with the roe attached, but occasionally in the shell. Prawns are often sold frozen, but can also be raw or cooked. It is best to buy them in the shell – look for firm flesh, and avoid any with black spots on the shells (except in the case of large black tiger prawns). Squid and octopus are sold fresh and frozen – the flesh shouldn't have any brown patches. Both smell foul if they are not fresh.

Make sure the packaging on sealed, smoked seafood isn't damaged and that the use-by date hasn't expired. If buying loose seafood, it shouldn't have an unpleasant smell or dry edges.

If salt cod is still flexible when you buy, wrap it in a damp towel and chill for up to three weeks; if it is rigid, wrap it in foil and chill for up to three months.

Always check the best-before dates on canned seafood.

Safe storage

Get your purchase home and refrigerated as soon as possible, ideally transporting it in an insulated bag.

Remove all packaging and clean the fish with a damp cloth, then wrap it in wet kitchen paper and place on a lipped plate at the bottom of the fridge, at a temperature no higher than 4°C/40°F.

Leave live clams, mussels and oysters in their bag. Do not put them in a bowl of water or a sealed container, as they will die. Store oysters in their shells, rounded cup down, covered with a wet cloth or some seaweed.

All shellfish should be stored in the bottom of the fridge and cooked or eaten within 12 hours. Fresh fish should also be cooked and eaten on the day of purchase, although most remain edible for another day if properly refrigerated. Oily fish spoils more quickly than white fish.

Refrigerate smoked or marinated seafood as soon as you get it home, and consume within two or three days, or by the use-by date.

Ways to cook fish

The Canadian Cooking Theory, developed some decades ago, advocates cooking fish for 10 minutes per 2.5 cm/1 inch at the thickest part for dry-heat methods. This is an easy approach for anyone new to seafood cooking, but many chefs today prefer 8–9 minutes for slightly less well-cooked fish. This is a matter of personal taste, so experiment and know how to tell when fish is cooked as you enjoy it: perfectly cooked fish is opaque with milky white juices and flakes and comes away from the bone easily; undercooked fish resists flaking, is translucent and has clear juices; overcooked fish looks dry and falls apart into thin pieces. Tuna and other meaty fish can be roasted and pan-seared like beef to be served rare, medium and well-done. When chargrilling, sautéing, pan- and stir-frying, start with a well-heated pan or wok, so that the fish develops a crust that retains internal moisture.

Dry-heat cooking – barbecuing, grilling, chargrilling and roasting

These are good methods for cooking whole fish, fillets, steaks and kebabs. Oily fish are well suited to grilling, barbecuing and chargrilling, because their natural oils baste the flesh, and their flavours are not overpowered by smoky aromas. Marinate white fish before barbecuing.

Barbecuing and grilling are similar, with the former cooking from the bottom and the latter from the top. In both cases, position the rack about 10 cm/4 inches from the heat. Brush the rack with oil, add the fish and cook until the flesh flakes easily, basting with a marinade or melted butter. Ideally cook without turning; if the surface is browning too quickly, adjust the rack position. Barbecue thin fillets and small fish, such as sardines, in a hinged fish basket.

Chargrilling is a quick way to give fish a barbecue flavour without having to light a barbecue. Heat a cast-iron griddle pan over a high heat, brush the fish with oil and chargrill until seared on one side and cooked through.

Whole fish are particularly delicious when roasted. Preheat the oven to 230°C/450°F/Gas Mark 8 and make a few slashes on each side. Rub the fish with oil, put in a roasting tin and roast, uncovered, until the flesh comes away from the bone when tested – the skin becomes crisp, while the flesh remains tenderly moist.

Wet-heat cooking – poaching, steaming and stewing

Fish is excellent poached or steamed. Although these techniques are very easy, they can still overcook fish so pay close attention. Another advantage is that the cooking liquid can be incorporated into a tasty sauce to serve alongside. Poach in gently simmering liquid flavoured with lemon and herbs for 8–12 minutes per 2.5 cm/1 inch of thickness. When steaming, make sure the seasoned fish never actually touches the water. Steam, covered, for 3–5 minutes for fillets and steaks and 8–9 minutes per 2.5 cm/1 inch of thickness for whole fish.

Sea fish stews often contain a variety of fish, simmered with other ingredients. To prevent overcooking, add the seafood towards the end, adding the most delicate pieces last – they will take only 2–3 minutes. Don't allow the liquid to boil.

Cooking in oil – sautéing, stir-frying and pan- and deep-frying

Fish steaks and fillets are most suited to these quick techniques. For sautéing and pan-frying, heat 5 mm/$^1/_4$ inch vegetable oil in a hot sauté or frying pan, dust the fish with seasoned flour and fry over medium–high heat for 2–3 minutes on each side for thin fillets, and up to 5–6 minutes for steaks 2.5 cm/1 inch thick.

Deep-frying requires fish to be coated in batter or crumbs and for the oil to be maintained at a steady 180°C/350°F. If you don't have a deep-fat fryer with a controlled thermostat, use a heavy-based saucepan and a thermometer: if the oil is too cool, the fried fish will be soggy; if it is too hot, the outside will be overcooked while the centre will be raw. Work in batches to prevent overcrowding and a reduction in the oil's temperature.

Roasted salmon

Serves 4

6 tbsp extra virgin olive oil

1 onion, sliced

1 leek, trimmed and sliced

juice of ½ lemon

2 tbsp chopped fresh parsley

2 tbsp chopped fresh dill

500 g/1 lb 2 oz salmon fillets

salt and pepper

freshly cooked baby spinach leaves and lemon wedges, to serve

Preheat the oven to 200°C/400°F/Gas Mark 6. Heat 1 tablespoon of the oil in a frying pan over a medium heat. Add the onion and leek and cook, stirring, for about 4 minutes until slightly soft.

Meanwhile, put the remaining oil in a small bowl with the lemon juice and herbs, and season with salt and pepper. Stir together well. Rinse the fish under cold running water, then pat dry with kitchen paper. Arrange the fish in a shallow, ovenproof baking dish.

Remove the frying pan from the heat and spread the onion and leek over the fish. Pour the oil mixture over the top, ensuring that everything is well coated. Roast in the centre of the preheated oven for about 10 minutes or until the fish is cooked through.

Arrange the cooked spinach on warmed serving plates. Remove the fish and vegetables from the oven and arrange on top of the spinach. Serve immediately, accompanied by the lemon wedges.

Tuna with green sauce

Serves 4

4 fresh tuna steaks, about 2 cm/¾ inch thick

olive oil, for brushing

salt and pepper

lemon wedges, to serve

Green sauce

55 g/2 oz fresh flat-leaf parsley, leaves and stems

4 spring onions, chopped

2 garlic cloves, chopped

3 anchovy fillets in oil, drained

30 g/1 oz fresh basil leaves

½ tbsp capers in brine, rinsed and dried

2 sprigs of fresh oregano or ½ tsp dried oregano

125 ml/4 fl oz extra virgin olive oil

1–2 tbsp lemon juice, to taste

To make the sauce, put the parsley, spring onions, garlic, anchovy fillets, basil, capers and oregano in a food processor. Pulse to chop and blend together. With the motor still running, pour in the oil through the feed tube. Add lemon juice to taste, then whiz again. If the sauce is too thick, add a little extra oil. Cover and chill until required.

Place a griddle pan over a high heat until you can feel the heat rising from the surface. Brush the tuna steaks with oil and place, oiled side down, on the hot pan and cook for 2 minutes.

Lightly brush the top side of the tuna steaks with a little more oil. Use a pair of tongs to turn over the tuna steaks, then season to taste with salt and pepper. Continue cooking for a further 2 minutes for rare or for up to 4 minutes for well done.

Transfer the tuna steaks to serving plates and serve with the sauce spooned over, accompanied by the lemon wedges.

Grilled swordfish with coriander & lime butter

Serves 4

corn oil, for brushing

4 swordfish steaks, about 175 g/6 oz each and 2.5 cm/1 inch thick

salt and pepper

fresh coriander leaves, to garnish

cherry tomatoes, to serve

Coriander & lime butter

125 g/4½ oz unsalted butter, softened

finely grated rind of 1 large lime

¼ tsp freshly squeezed lime juice

1 tbsp very finely shredded coriander leaves

pinch of ground cumin

To make the flavoured butter, put the butter into a bowl and beat until it is soft and smooth. Stir in the lime rind, lime juice, shredded coriander, cumin, and salt and pepper to taste. Spoon the butter onto a piece of greaseproof paper and roll into a log about 3 cm/1¼ inches thick. Refrigerate for at least 45 minutes or freeze until required.

When ready to cook the swordfish steaks, preheat the grill to high. Brush the grill rack with a little oil and position it about 10 cm/4 inches below the heat source.

Brush the steaks with oil and season to taste with salt and pepper. Put the steaks on the grill rack and cook for 4 minutes. Turn them over, then brush with a little more oil, season to taste with salt and pepper, and cook for a further 4–5 minutes, or until the fish is cooked and the flesh flakes easily.

Meanwhile, cut the butter into 8 equal slices. Transfer the steaks to individual plates. Put 2 slices of the butter on top of each steak and serve at once, garnished with the coriander leaves, accompanied by the cherry tomatoes.

Flaky pastry fish pie

Serves 6

- 650 g/1 lb 7 oz white fish fillets, such as cod or haddock, skinned
- 300 ml/10 fl oz milk
- 1 bay leaf
- 4 peppercorns
- 1 small onion, finely sliced
- 40 g/1½ oz butter, plus extra for greasing
- 40 g/1½ oz plain flour, plus extra for dusting
- 1 tbsp chopped fresh parsley or tarragon
- 150 ml/5 fl oz single cream
- 2 hard-boiled eggs, roughly chopped
- 400 g/14 oz ready-made puff pastry
- 1 egg, beaten
- salt and pepper

Preheat the oven to 200°C/400°F/Gas Mark 6. Grease a 1.2-litre/2-pint pie dish. Put the fish in a frying pan and cover with the milk. Add the bay leaf, peppercorns and onion slices. Bring to the boil, then reduce the heat and simmer gently for 10–12 minutes. Remove from the heat and strain the milk into a measuring jug. Add the remaining milk. Flake the fish into large pieces.

Melt the butter in a saucepan over a low heat, add the flour and cook, stirring constantly, for 2–3 minutes. Remove from the heat and gradually stir in the reserved milk, beating well after each addition. Return to the heat and cook, stirring until thick, smooth and glossy. Add the herbs, cream, and salt and pepper to taste.

Put the fish in the pie dish, add the hard-boiled eggs and season to taste with salt and pepper. Pour the sauce over the fish and mix carefully.

Roll out the pastry on a lightly floured work surface until just larger than the pie dish. Cut off a strip 1 cm/½ inch wide from around the edge. Moisten the rim of the dish with water and press the pastry strip onto it. Moisten the pastry collar and put on the pastry lid. Crimp the edges to seal well. Brush with the beaten egg. Put the pie on a baking tray and bake near the top of the preheated oven for 20–25 minutes. Remove from the oven and serve immediately.

Calamares

Serves 6

450 g/1 lb prepared squid

plain flour, for coating

sunflower oil, for deep-frying

salt

lemon wedges, to garnish

Aïoli (see page 23), to serve

Slice the squid into 1-cm/ ½-inch rings and halve the tentacles if large. Rinse under cold running water and dry well with kitchen paper. Dust the squid rings with flour so that they are lightly coated.

Heat the oil in a deep-fat fryer, large, heavy-based saucepan or wok to 180°C/ 350°F, or until a cube of bread browns in 30 seconds. Fry the squid rings in small batches for 2–3 minutes, or until golden brown and crisp all over, turning several times (if you fry too many squid rings at once, the oil temperature will drop and the rings will be soggy). Do not overcook as the squid will become tough and rubbery rather than moist and tender.

Remove with a slotted spoon and drain well on kitchen paper. Keep warm in a low oven while you fry the remaining squid rings.

Sprinkle the fried squid rings with salt and serve piping hot, garnished with lemon wedges for squeezing over. Accompany with a bowl of Aïoli for dipping.

Crab cakes

Makes 16

1 potato, peeled and cut into chunks

pinch of salt

4 spring onions, chopped

1 garlic clove, chopped

1 tbsp chopped fresh thyme

1 tbsp chopped fresh basil

1 tbsp chopped fresh coriander

225 g/8 oz white crabmeat, drained, if canned, and thawed, if frozen

½ tsp Dijon mustard

½ fresh green chilli, deseeded and finely chopped

1 egg, lightly beaten

plain flour, for dusting

sunflower oil, for shallow-frying

pepper

lime wedges, to garnish

salsa of your choice, to serve

Put the potato in a small saucepan, add water to cover and the salt. Bring to the boil, then reduce the heat, cover and simmer for 10–15 minutes until soft. Drain well, turn into a large bowl and mash with a potato masher or fork until smooth.

Meanwhile, put the spring onions, garlic, thyme, basil and coriander in a mortar and pound with a pestle until smooth. Add the herb paste to the mashed potato with the crabmeat, mustard, chilli, egg, and pepper to taste. Mix well, cover with clingfilm and chill in the refrigerator for 30 minutes.

Sprinkle flour onto a large, flat plate. Shape spoonfuls of the crabmeat mixture into small balls with your hands, then flatten slightly and dust with flour, shaking off any excess. Heat the oil in a frying pan over a high heat, add the crab cakes and cook in batches for 2–3 minutes on each side until golden. Remove with a slotted spoon and drain on kitchen paper. Set aside to cool to room temperature.

Arrange the crab cakes on a serving dish, garnish with the lime wedges and serve with a bowl of salsa.

My special recipes

Notes

My special recipes

Notes

My special recipes

Notes

My special recipes

Notes

My special recipes

Notes

My special recipes

Notes

Sweet & baked

Getting started

EQUIPMENT

Measuring scales, mixing bowls, a wooden spoon, a few baking tins and a rolling pin are all the items you need to begin baking. But as the baking bug bites, you can gradually add other tools to those basics, such as an electric whisk and a food processor, which, although not essential, will certainly make the job easier and quicker.

Measuring

For successful baking, it is essential to have accurate measuring scales or cups and a set of measuring spoons. Electronic or balance scales are more accurate than measuring cups, which measure ingredients by volume. If you intend to do a lot of baking but generally use cups for measuring, it is worth investing in a set of scales to ensure success every time. It is important to bear in mind that spoon measures are always level unless otherwise stated in the recipe.

Mixing, beating and blending

Bowls: You will need a selection of bowls of various sizes. Choose from ceramic, glass or stainless steel.

Spoons: Wooden spoons come in a variety of sizes and are essential for beating ingredients together.
A large metal spoon is useful for folding in flour.

Spatulas: Plastic or silicone spatulas are ideal for scraping out bowls with the minimum of waste, as well as for folding in flour.

Electric whisks and mixers: Electric appliances take the hard work out of creaming and whisking cake mixtures. A hand-held electric whisk is sufficient for cakes, while a free-standing mixer is useful for those who like to bake in larger quantities and for making bread. A manual balloon whisk is good for whisking egg whites and sponge mixes.

Food processors: These are good for rubbing fat into flour quickly and efficiently. They can also be used to prepare cake mixtures, but tend not to incorporate as much air as mixing by hand or with a whisk, so the cake may be more dense.

Bakeware

It is advisable to invest in a few good-quality baking tins. If looked after, they will last a lifetime, and are less likely than inexpensive tins to twist or buckle in the oven and to cause sticking or burning. Choose ones that feel relatively heavy and do not bend easily.
The most useful to begin with are:

- Baking sheets
- 18-cm/7-inch shallow cake tins
- 20-cm/8-inch shallow cake tins
- 23-cm/9-inch shallow cake tins
- 20-cm/8-inch deep loose-based or springform tin
- 20-cm/8-inch square cake tin
- 450-g/1-lb and 900-g/2-lb loaf tins
- 12-hole muffin and bun tins
- Swiss roll tin
- 20-cm/8-inch flan tin

INGREDIENTS

Flour

Wheat flour is the most commonly used flour for baking. The amount of gluten (protein) in wheat flour varies between the different types:

- Plain white flour has the bran and wheat germ removed, and is then fortified with vitamins. Soft plain flour, made from wheat with a low gluten content, has a fine texture and is ideal for making cakes, pastry and biscuits. Strong plain flour is milled from wheat with a high gluten content and is used for breads and most yeast cookery.
- Self-raising flour is plain white flour with baking powder added as a raising agent. To make your own self-raising flour add 2 teaspoons of baking powder to each 225 g/8 oz plain flour.
- Wholemeal flour is flour that has been milled from the whole of the wheat grain. It is coarser and heavier than white flour. It is available as a strong (high-gluten) flour for bread making and a soft (lower-gluten) flour for cakes and pastry.
- Other flours, such as brown flour, malted flour, cornflour and

buckwheat, rye, rice and chestnut flours, are also sometimes used to a limited extent in baking, each having its own unique flavour.

Sugars

Most sugar is produced from one of two sources: sugar cane or sugar beet. There are several different types of sugar, each with its own particular qualities. Unrefined sugars are made from sugar cane and have a higher mineral, vitamin and trace element content than refined sugars.

- Granulated sugar can be used to achieve a crunchy texture in some biscuits and in cakes prepared by the rubbing-in method.
- Caster sugar has a finer crystal and dissolves more readily. It is the type of sugar most frequently used in baking. It is known as caster sugar because it is suitable for placing in a caster – a container with a perforated top, similar to a flour dredger.
- Golden granulated, golden caster and golden icing sugar are the unrefined forms of the refined sugars.
- Molasses sugar is a dark, fine-grained unrefined sugar with a strong flavour, used for rich fruit cakes.
- Dark muscovado sugar is an unrefined sugar that has a less intense flavour than molasses sugar, but a good, dark colour. It is ideal for light fruit cakes and gingerbread.
- Light muscovado sugar is lighter in colour and flavour than the dark variety and is used widely in cakes, muffins, tea breads and biscuits.
- Demerara sugar is a large, coarse-grained brown sugar that can be made from either refined or unrefined sugar. As well as being used in baking, it is sometimes sprinkled over the tops of pies, crumbles and cakes for its crunchy texture.
- Soft light and dark brown sugars are similar to light and dark muscovado sugars. They are usually refined white sugar that has been tossed in molasses or syrup.
- Icing sugar has a very fine, powdery grain and dissolves almost instantly. It is used in some biscuits and pastry, and for making icings and fillings.

Fats

- Butter produces the best flavour. Unsalted butter is generally considered best for baking. If you do use salted butter, you will not need to add any extra salt to the recipe (except for bread making). Use butter straight from the refrigerator for pastry making and at room temperature for cake making.
- Some people prefer margarine over butter for baking. Block margarine is generally the best, but soft tub margarine is needed for making cakes by the all-in-one method.
- Low-fat spreads are not suitable for baking, as they contain a high proportion of water.
- Suet is used for making suet crust pastry and can be made from either shredded beef fat or solidified vegetable oils.
- Lard and white vegetable fat have a bland flavour, but give a light, short texture to pastry and biscuits, so are sometimes used. They are usually combined with butter for flavour.

Eggs

The size of egg used is important. Store eggs in the refrigerator away from strong-smelling foods. Remove from the refrigerator to return to room temperature before using if possible, as cold eggs do not combine as well with other ingredients or trap as much air.

Raising agents

- Baking powder is a mixture of cream of tartar and bicarbonate of soda. When mixed with moisture, it releases carbon dioxide, a harmless gas that expands during baking to make the food rise.
- Bicarbonate of soda produces carbon dioxide when mixed with an acid such as lemon juice or buttermilk.
- Yeast is a single-cell organism that converts the natural sugars in flour to produce carbon dioxide. Yeast needs warmth, moisture and food (sugars) to work. It is available in both dried and fresh forms for baking.

Baking tips

Greasing and lining cake tins

Unless you have non-stick bakeware, you will need to grease your baking tins before using, and you may prefer to take the extra precaution of greasing non-stick tins in any case. A little butter or margarine can be smeared onto the tin, or a light-flavoured oil can be brushed over the entire inside surface with a pastry brush to give a very light coating. Some recipes require the baking tin to be lined. In some cases, only the base of the tin needs to be lined, which helps to ensure that the cake is successfully turned out. Use greaseproof paper or non-stick baking paper to line the tins.

Lining a round cake tin: Place the tin on the paper and draw around it. Cut out the round just inside the drawn line. Cut a strip of paper about 2 cm/¾ inch wider than the depth of the tin and long enough to go around the tin. Fold over about 1 cm/½ inch along one long edge and snip from the edge up to the fold at 2-cm/¾-inch intervals along the length. Lightly grease the tin and position the strip of paper around the edge so that the snipped edge lies flat on the base of the tin. Lay the disc of paper in the base and lightly grease.

For rich fruit cakes, extra protection is needed to prevent the edges from burning or drying out during the extended cooking time. Line the tin as above, but use a double thickness of paper. Cut a double-thickness strip of brown paper about 2 cm/¾ inch deeper than the tin. Wrap around the outside of the tin and secure with string.

Lining a shallow or swiss roll tin: Cut the paper about 7.5 cm/3 inches longer and wider than the tin. Lightly grease the tin and place the paper on top. Snip at the corners and press into the tin. Lightly grease the paper.

Lining a loaf tin: Lightly grease the tin. Cut two strips of paper, one the width of the tin and long enough to cover the sides and base, and one the length of the tin and long enough to cover the base and sides. Press each piece into place and lightly grease.

Is it cooked?

Follow the timings in the recipe as a guideline, but also rely on your own judgement, as ovens vary in temperature. Small cakes should be well risen, firm and springy to the touch, and sponge cakes should also be springy to the touch. Test by gently pressing the cake with a finger. Once you have removed your finger, the cake should spring back, but if you can still see the fingerprint, return the cake to the oven for a few minutes longer. Fruit cake and deep sponge cakes are best tested with a skewer inserted into the centre. The skewer should come out clean when the cake is cooked.

For most cakes, leave to cool for a few minutes in the tin before turning out and transferring to a wire rack to cool completely. Some cakes, such as rich fruit cakes, benefit from being allowed to cool completely in the tin.

Baking blind

When used to line a tin, shortcrust pastry is often precooked to set the pastry before the filling is added.

Line the tin with the rolled-out pastry and prick the base with a fork. Chill for about 30 minutes in the refrigerator or 10 minutes in the freezer (you can also bake pastry cases blind from frozen).

Line the pastry case with a sheet of non-stick baking paper, greaseproof paper or foil and fill with purpose-made ceramic or metal baking beans or dried pulses or rice. Bake for 10 minutes, then remove the paper and beans and bake for a further 10 minutes until the pastry is just golden. Remove from the oven and brush a little beaten egg or egg white over the base to seal.

What went wrong?

Accurate measuring and careful following of the recipe should ensure success. However, when things do go wrong, there is often a simple reason, and if you identify the cause, the mistake can be avoided in the future.

CAKES

Sunk in the middle

- Cake slightly undercooked
- Oven door opened too early
- Mixture too wet
- Over-beating of the fat and sugar
- Too much raising agent
- Oven temperature too low

Unevenly risen

- Mixture not spread in tin evenly
- Flour not folded in evenly (whisked sponges)
- Oven not properly preheated
- Oven or oven shelves not level

Peaked or cracked top

- Baking in too hot an oven
- Too much mixture in the tin
- Too much raising agent
- Mixture too wet or too dry
- Cooking too near the top of the oven

Crust too pale

- Cake cooked too low in the oven
- Oven overloaded
- Oven too cool

Crust too dark

- Cake cooked too near the top of the oven
- Oven temperature too high
- Tin too large
- Baked too long

Speckled top

- Insufficient beating of fat and sugar
- Granulated or demerara sugar used

SHORTCRUST PASTRY

Difficult to roll

- Too dry
- Self-raising flour used instead of plain flour
- Too much fat
- Over-mixed

Excessive shrinking

- Over-handling
- Pastry stretched when rolling
- Not allowing pastry to rest before baking

Soggy

- Not fully cooked
- Too much liquid
- Pie cover placed over hot filling
- No vent for steam to escape (pies)
- Filling poured into pastry case that has cracks or holes

Hard or tough pastry

- Over-handling
- Too little fat
- Too much liquid
- Oven temperature too low

Blistered crust

- Water not evenly mixed in
- Fat not properly rubbed in

BREAD

Insufficiently risen

- Too little yeast
- Too little sugar
- Too much salt
- Yeast out of date
- Insufficient time proving
- Proving at too low a temperature

Risen too much

- Too much yeast
- Too little salt

Sunk in the centre

- Too much liquid
- Too little salt
- Too much yeast
- Over-proving

Centre soggy

- Too much of the wet ingredients/ water
- Oven temperature too high

Damp crust

- Left in the tin too long after baking
- Wrapped while warm

Crust too dark

- Too much sugar
- Cooked too long or at too high a temperature

Dense texture

- Not enough liquid
- Soft flour used
- Insufficient kneading
- Too much salt
- Liquid too hot (kills the yeast)
- Grains without sufficient gluten used

Coarse, open texture

- Too much liquid
- Over-proving
- Oven temperature too low

Flat top

- Flour too soft
- Dough too wet

Victoria sandwich

Makes 8–10 slices

175 g/6 oz butter, at room temperature, plus extra for greasing

175 g/6 oz caster sugar

3 eggs, beaten

175 g/6 oz self-raising flour

pinch of salt

3 tbsp raspberry jam

1 tbsp caster or icing sugar

Preheat the oven to 180°C/350°F/Gas Mark 4. Grease 2 x 20-cm/8-inch round shallow cake tins and base-line with greaseproof or non-stick baking paper.

Cream the butter and sugar together in a bowl until pale and fluffy. Add the eggs, a little at a time, beating well after each addition.

Sift the flour and salt together, then gently fold into the mixture using a metal spoon or a spatula. Divide the mixture between the prepared tins and smooth the surfaces.

Bake both cakes on the same shelf in the centre of the preheated oven for 25–30 minutes until well risen, golden brown and beginning to shrink from the side of each tin.

Leave to stand in the tins for 1 minute. Using a palette knife, loosen the cakes from around the edge of each tin. Turn out the cakes onto a clean tea towel, remove the lining paper and invert onto a wire rack (this prevents the rack marking the top of the cakes).

When completely cool, sandwich together with the jam and sprinkle with the sugar. The cake is delicious when freshly baked, but any remaining cake can be stored in an airtight tin for up to 1 week.

Mississippi mud pie

Serves 8

Pastry

225 g/8 oz plain flour, plus extra for dusting
2 tbsp cocoa powder
140 g/5 oz butter
2 tbsp caster sugar
1–2 tbsp cold water

Filling

175 g/6 oz butter
350 g/12 oz soft dark brown sugar
4 eggs, lightly beaten
4 tbsp cocoa powder, sifted
150 g/5½ oz plain chocolate, broken into pieces
300 ml/10 fl oz single cream
1 tsp chocolate essence

To decorate

425 ml/15 fl oz double cream, whipped
chocolate flakes and curls

To make the pastry, sift the flour and cocoa powder into a mixing bowl. Rub in the butter with the fingertips until the mixture resembles fine breadcrumbs. Stir in the sugar and enough cold water to mix to a soft dough. Wrap the dough in clingfilm and chill in the refrigerator for 15 minutes.

Preheat the oven to 190°C/375°F/Gas Mark 5. Roll out the pastry on a lightly floured work surface and use to line a 23-cm/9-inch loose-based flan tin or ceramic flan dish. Line with greaseproof paper and fill with baking beans. Bake in the preheated oven for 15 minutes. Remove the paper and beans from the pastry case and cook for a further 10 minutes until crisp.

To make the filling, beat the butter and sugar together in a bowl and gradually beat in the eggs with the cocoa powder. Melt the chocolate and beat it into the mixture with the cream and the chocolate essence.

Reduce the oven temperature to 160°C/325°F/Gas Mark 3. Pour the mixture into the pastry case and bake for 45 minutes, or until the filling has set gently.

Let the mud pie cool completely, then transfer the pie to a serving plate. Cover with the whipped cream. Decorate the pie with chocolate flakes and curls and then chill until ready to serve.

Traditional apple pie

Serves 6

Pastry

350 g/12 oz plain flour

pinch of salt

85 g/3 oz butter or margarine, cut into small pieces

85 g/3 oz white vegetable fat, cut into small pieces

about 6 tbsp cold water

beaten egg or milk, for glazing

Filling

1 kg/2 lb 4 oz cooking apples, peeled, cored and sliced

125 g/4½ oz brown or white sugar, plus extra for sprinkling

½–1 tsp ground cinnamon, mixed spice or ground ginger

1–2 tbsp water (optional)

Preheat the oven to 220°C/425°F/Gas Mark 7. To make the pastry, sift the flour and salt into a mixing bowl. Add the butter and vegetable fat and rub in with your fingertips until the mixture resembles fine breadcrumbs. Add the water and gather the mixture together into a pastry. Wrap the pastry and chill for 30 minutes. Thinly roll out almost two thirds of the pastry and use to line a 20–23-cm/ 8–9-inch deep pie dish or shallow pie tin.

Mix the apples with the sugar and spice and pack into the pastry case; the filling can come up above the rim. Add the water, if necessary.

Roll out the remaining pastry to form a lid. Dampen the edges of the pie rim with water and position the lid, pressing the edges together firmly. Trim and crimp the edges. Use the trimmings to cut out leaves or other shapes to decorate the top of the pie, dampen and attach. Glaze the top of the pie with beaten egg or milk, make 1–2 slits in the top, and put the pie dish on a baking tray.

Bake in the preheated oven for 20 minutes, then reduce the temperature to 180°C/350°F/Gas Mark 4 and cook for 30 minutes until the pastry is a light golden brown. Serve hot or cold, sprinkled with sugar.

Double chocolate chip cookies

Makes 24

200 g/7 oz butter, softened, plus extra for greasing

200 g/7 oz caster sugar

½ tsp vanilla extract

1 large egg

225 g/8 oz plain flour

pinch of salt

1 tsp bicarbonate of soda

115 g/4 oz white chocolate chips

115 g/4 oz plain chocolate chips

Preheat the oven to 180°C/350°F/Gas Mark 4. Grease 2 baking sheets with butter. Place the butter, sugar and vanilla extract in a large bowl and beat together. Gradually beat in the egg until the mixture is light and fluffy.

Sift the flour, salt and bicarbonate of soda over the mixture and fold in. Fold in the chocolate chips.

Drop heaped teaspoonfuls of the mixture on to the prepared baking sheets, allowing room for the cookies to spread during cooking. Bake in the preheated oven for 10–12 minutes, or until crisp outside but still soft inside. Leave to cool on the baking sheets for 2 minutes, then transfer to wire racks to cool completely.

Scones

Makes 10–12

55 g/2 oz butter, diced and chilled, plus extra for greasing

450 g/1 lb plain flour, plus extra for dusting

½ tsp salt

2 tsp baking powder

2 tbsp caster sugar

250 ml/9 fl oz milk, plus 3 tbsp for glazing

clotted cream and strawberry jam, to serve

Preheat the oven to 220°C/425°F/Gas Mark 7. Grease a baking sheet with a little butter.

Sift the flour, salt and baking powder together into a bowl. Rub in the butter with your fingertips until the mixture resembles fine breadcrumbs. Stir in the sugar. Make a well in the centre and pour in the milk. Quickly mix with a round-bladed knife to form a soft dough.

Turn out the dough onto a lightly floured work surface and knead lightly. Roll out to a thickness of about 1 cm/½ inch. Don't be heavy-handed – scones need a light touch. Using a plain 6-cm/2½-inch biscuit cutter, cut out 10–12 rounds and transfer to the prepared baking sheet.

Brush with the milk to glaze and bake in the preheated oven for 10–12 minutes until well risen and golden.

Transfer to a wire rack and leave to cool. Split and serve with clotted cream and strawberry jam.

New York cheesecake

Serves 8–10

sunflower oil, for brushing

85 g/3 oz butter

200 g/7 oz digestive biscuits, crushed

400 g/14 oz cream cheese

2 large eggs

140 g/5 oz caster sugar

1½ tsp vanilla extract

450 ml/16 fl oz soured cream

Blueberry topping

55 g/2 oz caster sugar

4 tbsp water

250 g/9 oz fresh blueberries

1 tsp arrowroot

Preheat the oven to 190°C/375°F/Gas Mark 5. Brush a 20-cm/8-inch springform tin with oil. Melt the butter in a saucepan over a low heat. Stir in the biscuits, then spread the mixture over the base of the tin. Place the cream cheese, eggs, 100 g/3½ oz of the sugar and ½ teaspoon of the vanilla extract in a food processor. Process until smooth. Pour over the biscuit base and smooth the top. Place on a baking tray and bake for 20 minutes until set. Remove from the oven and set aside for 20 minutes. Leave the oven switched on.

Mix the cream with the remaining sugar and vanilla extract in a bowl. Spoon over the cheesecake. Return it to the oven for 10 minutes, leave to cool, then cover with clingfilm and chill in the refrigerator for 8 hours, or overnight.

To make the topping, place the sugar in a saucepan with 2 tablespoons of the water over a low heat and stir until the sugar has dissolved. Increase the heat, add the blueberries, cover and cook for a few minutes, or until they begin to soften. Remove from the heat. Mix the arrowroot and remaining water in a bowl, add to the fruit and stir until smooth. Return to a low heat. Cook until the juice thickens and turns translucent. Leave to cool.

Remove the cheesecake from the tin 1 hour before serving. Spoon the topping over and chill until ready to serve.

White bread

Makes 1 large loaf or 8 rolls

butter, for greasing

450 g/1 lb strong white bread flour, plus extra for dusting

1 tsp salt

1½ tsp easy-blend dried yeast

1 tbsp vegetable oil, plus extra for oiling

350 ml/12 fl oz hand-hot water

Grease a 900-g/2-lb loaf tin or 2 baking sheets. Sift the flour and salt together into a large warmed bowl. Stir in the yeast. Make a well in the centre. Add the oil and water to the well and mix to form a soft dough.

Turn out the dough onto a lightly floured work surface and knead for 5–10 minutes, or until smooth and elastic. Put the dough in an oiled bowl, cover with clingfilm and leave to rise in a warm place for 1 hour, or until doubled in size.

Turn out the dough again and knead lightly. For a loaf, shape into a rectangle the length of the tin and 3 times the width. With the long sides facing you, fold the top one-third down to cover the middle third, then fold the bottom one-third up and over the top and press together. Transfer to the prepared tin, join-side down. Alternatively, to make rolls, cut the dough into 8 equal pieces, shape each piece into a round and space well apart on the prepared baking sheets. Dust with a little extra flour for a softer crust. Cover and leave to prove in a warm place for 30 minutes, or until the loaf is well risen above the tin or the rolls have doubled in size. Preheat the oven to 230°C/450°F/Gas Mark 8.

If baking a loaf, bake in the centre of the preheated oven for 25–30 minutes, or until it sounds hollow when tapped on the base. If the top is browning too much, reduce the temperature a little. For the rolls, bake for 15–20 minutes, swapping the baking sheets around halfway through the baking time. Transfer to a wire rack and leave to cool.

Mixed seed bread

Makes 1 loaf

butter, for greasing

375 g/13 oz strong white bread flour, plus extra for dusting

125 g/4½ oz rye flour

1½ tsp salt

1 tsp easy-blend dried yeast

1 tbsp light brown sugar

1½ tbsp skimmed milk powder

1 tsp caraway seeds

½ tsp poppy seeds

½ tsp sesame seeds

300 ml/10 fl oz hand-hot water

1½ tbsp sunflower oil, plus extra for oiling

2 tsp lemon juice

Topping

1 egg white

1 tbsp water

1 tbsp sunflower or pumpkin seeds

Grease a 900-g/2-lb loaf tin. Sift the flours and salt together into a large warmed bowl. Stir in the yeast, sugar, milk powder and seeds. Make a well in the centre. Mix the water, oil and lemon juice together and add to the well. Mix to form a dough.

Turn out the dough onto a lightly floured work surface and knead for 5–10 minutes, or until smooth and elastic. Put the dough into an oiled bowl, cover with clingfilm and leave to rise in a warm place for 1 hour, or until doubled in size.

Turn out the dough again and knead lightly. Shape into a loaf and transfer to the prepared tin. Cover and leave to prove in a warm place for 30 minutes. Preheat the oven to 220°C/425°F/Gas Mark 7.

To make the topping, lightly beat the egg white with the water. Brush over the top of the loaf, then gently press the seeds all over the top. Bake in the preheated oven for 25–30 minutes, or until it sounds hollow when tapped on the base. Transfer to a wire rack and leave to cool.

My special recipes

Notes

My special recipes

Notes

My special recipes

Notes

My special recipes

Notes

My special recipes

Notes

My special recipes

Notes

index

index

index